PETER V. MACDONALD

HILARIOUS TALES
FROM OUR MEN AND WOMEN
OF THE BADGE

Published in 1996 by
Stoddart Publishing Co. Limited
34 Lesmill Road
Toronto, Canada
M3B 2T6
Tel. (416) 445-3333
Fax (416) 445-5967

Stoddart Books are available for bulk purchase for sales promotions,
premiums, fundraising, and seminars. For details, contact the
Special Sales Department at the above address.

Canadian Cataloguing in Publication Data

MacDonald, Peter V. (Peter Vincent), 1934 –
From the cop shop: hilarious tales
from our men and women of the badge

ISBN: 0-7737-2912-7

1. Police – Anecdotes. 2. Police – Humor.
3. Crime – Anecdotes. 4. Crime – Humor.
5. Canadian wit and humor (English).• I. Title.

HV7914.M33 1995   363.2'0207   C95-931227-7

Cover Design: Bill Douglas/The Bang
Text Design: Tannice Goddard
Printed and bound in Canada

Stoddart Publishing gratefully acknowledges the support
of the Canada Council, the Ontario Ministry of Citizenship,
Culture and Recreation, Ontario Arts Council, and Ontario
Publishing Centre in the development of
writing and publishing in Canada.

To police officers everywhere —
courageous warriors who put their lives on the line
every time they show up for work

Contents

Preface

I have always depended on the kindness of strangers.
— Tennessee Williams

As I worked on this book it struck me that the foregoing famous line, delivered by Blanche Dubois in *A Streetcar Named Desire*, describes perfectly what I've been doing for the past dozen years or so.

In all three of my bestselling books on legal humour — *Court Jesters, More Court Jesters*, and *Return of the Court Jesters* — I depended on the kindness of strangers, who bombarded me with about twelve hundred true, humorous yarns. And now, glutton that I am, I've done it all over again — this time in the allied field of police work. I'm delighted to report that the kindness of strangers has produced yet another bumper crop of funny true-life tales — from thirteen countries.

A cop's job is packed with tension and is at all times highly dangerous. Indeed, the possibility of death lurks around every corner. But that doesn't mean police officers deal only with gloom, doom, and disaster in the course of their daily duties. Nor does it mean that these protectors of the public peace never encounter an amusing situation, or hear a funny remark, or crack off a humorous line of their own, while on their appointed rounds. In fact, such on-the-job delights are quite common in their line of work.

As my *Court Jesters* books demonstrated over and over again, laughter is an invaluable tension-breaker, which some fortunate folks can flip on and off like a light switch. In this sad old world, having a sense of humour helps tremendously in enabling one to retain one's marbles.

"Against the assault of laughter nothing can stand," noted Mark Twain. And Mary Pettibone Poole put it even more succinctly: "He who laughs, lasts."

This is doubly true in police work, where humour is a great coping mechanism — a whistling-past-the-graveyard sort of mockery of one's fear of death that makes life bearable. As a cop friend of mine once told me, "The salvation of a police officer is his or her sense of humour. There are so many occasions in this job when, if you didn't laugh, you'd cry. Out of earshot of victims and witnesses, we can find something funny about almost any situation except the death of children."

Retired police sergeant Samuel Hill, of Coleraine, Northern Ireland, wrote me and said: "Whether investigating a case of burglary, refereeing at a drunken party, sorting out the imaginary fears of a lonely old person, or whatever, a police officer's sense of humour is often the saving grace that enables him or her to keep going."

Then, putting in a well-deserved plug for coppers everywhere, Sam noted: "Chasing and catching criminals is only part of our work. Less spectacular — but even more valuable — is the quiet, steady work of protecting the great mass of law-abiding people and helping them to live a happy and secure life."

I believe this book is unique. A great many volumes have been written about the serious side of police work, and some of them have even contained a few funny tales. But as far as I can tell from sifting through stacks of *Books in Print* directories, no one but yours truly has written and published a book devoted *entirely* to the telling of humorous anecdotes that have arisen in the course of police work around the world. Hordes of wonderful people who sent me stories for this new undertaking said they were extremely pleased that someone was "finally" doing this.

• • •

While researching and writing this book I made many new friends — by letter, fax, and phone — in Canada, the United States, Bermuda, the United Kingdom, Ireland, Australia, Europe, and India. I wish to thank everyone who took the time and trouble to send me funny stories and tips as to where to find others — especially the following highly industrious contributors: my longtime friend, Police Sergeant Gary Dale, of Port Elgin, Ontario, who several years ago convinced me I should branch out into the wacky world of police humour; Inspector Eric Fiander and Sergeant Eric Carr of the Fredericton, New Brunswick, police force; ex-cop Morley S. Lymburner, editor and publisher of *Blue Line* magazine, Markham, Ontario; lawyer, historian, and raconteur David N. Muise, of Sydney, Nova Scotia; RCMP constable Jack MacNeill, of Charlottetown, Prince Edward Island; RCMP constable Duncan Chisholm, of Deer Lake, Newfoundland; former Scotland Yard sleuth Hughie Brown, of Regina, Saskatchewan; Noela Bamford, of Regina, Saskatchewan; Delphine Richards, of Carmarthen, Dyfed, Wales; Cheryl Ann Pratt, of Moab, Utah; former Windsor, Ontario, policeman Al Porter, of Detroit, Michigan; and Detective Terry L. Davis, of Lemoore, California.

Extra-special thanks are reserved for my dear wife, Catherine, who, as in previous book ventures, helped me cheerfully, constantly, and in countless ways. Special thanks go to my sons,

Michael and Shaun; my daughter, Mary MacDonald Savides; and my son-in-law, Paris Savides. (And, come to think of it, to the two gorgeous children they added to the family tree while this book was in progress, to wit, Alexander MacDonald Savides and Cleo MacDonald Savides.)

And now, without further ado, let's see what goodies the kind strangers have sent for our amusement.

PETER V. MACDONALD
Hanover, Ontario

1

STUPID CROOKS

If a thing's worth doing, it's worth doing badly.
— G.K. Chesterton

You're about to meet dozens of nitwits and nincompoops who've failed miserably at crime, and have in the process brightened the lives of countless cops. Doctors the world over have confirmed that laughing can be extremely good for whatever ails you. So let's trot out some of these bozos and hope they can cheer us up, too.

On a busy Friday evening in 1977 Constable Gary Dale of Hanover, Ontario, had some unforgettable dealings with a particularly stupid crook.

The drama began when he responded to a call from a camera shop. A 35-mm camera and flash unit had been stolen by a shady-looking character in a black trenchcoat.

Gary got a detailed description of the merchandise and the cad who'd swiped it. Then the saleswoman said, "Would you like a picture of the thief?"

"How come you have a picture of him?" a flabbergasted Gary inquired.

The clerk said the man in the trenchcoat had shown interest in the 35-mm and flash, but then started asking questions about a Polaroid she was loading with film.

She told him that Polaroids were quite the thing, producing sharp colour pictures in a matter of seconds.

"Would you like a demonstration?" she asked the fellow.

"Sure, why not?" he replied, and the clerk snapped his picture. When she bent her head to pull the photo out of the camera, he grabbed the 35-mm camera and flash and ran out of the store.

The constable took one look at the snazzy new photograph and immediately recognized a man we'll call Sammy Schultz.

"Thanks for the picture," Gary told the clerk. "I bet I know where this fellow is right now."

He made a beeline for the Queen's Hotel, about a block down the street, and sure enough, there was Sammy, swigging beer with one of his pals.

When Gary Dale approached and waved the Polaroid photo in his face, Sammy knew the jig was up. Sullenly and resignedly, he fished the camera from one of the pockets of his trenchcoat.

"Come on, Sammy," said Constable Dale, "let's have the rest of it, too."

"Aw, shit, Gary," moaned the bungler, reaching down into the crotch of his pants and retrieving the flash unit.

Pulverized by a Polaroid, Sammy Schultz pleaded guilty to a charge of theft and was levied a hefty fine. As for Gary Dale, who'd nailed him in three minutes, he laughed on and off for the next three days.

• • •

According to historians, who should know, history is constantly repeating itself. You'd better believe it.

One night in 1989 two youths broke into a Saskatoon office and pawed through a filing cabinet, where they came across a Polaroid camera. Not wanting to steal defective goods, they tested it right then and there by taking snapshots of themselves.

The camera worked perfectly. The pictures were tossed in the waste basket, where the police found them the next morning. They led to immediate arrests.

• • •

Constable Brian Jack of the RCMP detachment in Powerview, Manitoba, can top that tale.

In August 1993 Brian and another Mountie recovered a car, three rifles, two shotguns, mounds of ammunition, numerous bottles of booze, and a zillion other items that had been stolen from the trailer of a local man.

"During the search several empty Polaroid film boxes and used film cartridges were found," Constable Jack reports. "We wondered if the thieves had been so dumb as to take pictures of themselves to assist us. Sure enough, while piling up three car-loads of goods we came across a shaving kit that contained a bundle of Polaroids.

"These shots were very candid and showed four youths in the stolen car, shooting the weapons, drinking the liquor, and generally having a good time. The photos triggered a lot of laughter — and led to the speedy arrest of the culprits."

• • •

About fifteen years ago in Port Elgin, Ontario, a chap who was running low on cash decided to hold up a bank in Hamilton, a hundred miles or so down the road. He pulled off the heist

3

without a hitch, then jumped into his car and sped away, his pockets crammed with cash. Very soon thereafter, police arrived at the bank and obtained a description of the culprit and the licence number of his vehicle.

The robber, meanwhile, had pulled into the parking lot of a nearby bar and gone in to hoist a few until the heat was off. In a matter of minutes the cops located his car, as well as some drugs that were stashed therein, and towed the vehicle to police headquarters.

When the fugitive left the bar he discovered his car was gone. He went back inside, phoned the police, told them where he was calling from, and reported that his vehicle had been stolen.

"Stay there," he was told. "We'll be right down to interview you."

The crook ordered another drink but before he could finish it he was under arrest for bank robbery.

• • •

In Vancouver, British Columbia, in 1984, a young bank teller gave police a vivid description of a real pro at work. She said a man stood in line, patiently waiting his turn, and as soon as he reached her wicket he growled, "This is a holdup. Give me all your money."

The teller was puzzled. "Where's your gun?" she inquired.

"My friend's got it, and he'll use it," the man assured her.

"Where's your friend?" she asked.

"He's at the back of the line," the bandit replied.

"What's he wearing?"

"A brown jacket."

The woman scanned the lineup, then said, "He's gone."

"Well, give me the money anyway," the flustered fellow demanded.

"Wait right here," said the teller. "I have to ask my boss."

She vanished into an office, then seconds later returned and told the robber, "You can only have $150."

"That'll do," he said quickly, then grabbed the meagre offering and scooted towards the door.

He was greeted by two policemen, who escorted him to head-quarters.

"New at this?" one of the officers asked as they drove off.

"Yes," the man sighed, "it's my first time."

• • •

Several years ago Judge Spyros Loukidelis of Sudbury, Ontario, wrote to me about a couple of stickup "artists" who were prosecuted by a friend of his in British Columbia:

Two robbers drove into a small shopping plaza. They got out of their car and crouched down behind it to put on stocking masks. When they stood up they realized they had their masks on backwards.

They eventually solved that problem and went into a Singer Sewing Centre and announced that this was a bank robbery. The lady told them that the bank was two doors down. They thanked her and headed into the bank.

One of them stood guard, and his partner explained to a young teller that this was a robbery and they wanted money. She fearfully complied. He then looked around and said to the teller that the bag to carry the loot in had been left in the car and would she please lend them a bag. Again she complied.

The two rushed out of the bank and the alarm was set off by the staff. The man who'd got the money had to return, as he'd left the car keys on the counter. He then rushed out to join his companion just as the police arrived. There was a shootout and one of the two was wounded before they surrendered.

• • •

When it comes to botched stickups, it's hard to beat this one.

In 1988 a Toronto man with forty-four previous convictions, many of them for robbery, was found guilty of holding up a bank. The note he'd handed the teller was short and (like its author) punchy: "This is a up."

5

The judge sent him up — the river, that is — for three years.

• • •

In 1994 a twenty-five-year-old man named Paul Kimball was charged with sexual assault in Ogden, Utah. The alleged culprit escaped but was apprehended easily because he'd left the victim's house without his pants, which contained his wallet and all sorts of identification.

• • •

Former Windsor, Ontario, policeman Al Porter has stories galore about his years on the force. Here's a sample:

One evening about ten years ago Windsor detective Ted Willis and his wife went out for a while. Shortly after they left, a neighbour, who could see their place from his, a klutzy criminal we'll call Joe Smith, went over and broke into the Willis place.

Immediately Ted's dog grabbed the seat of Smith's pants with his teeth and ripped off a big chunk thereof. With that, Smith hightailed it for home.

When Ted and his wife returned and learned that their house had been broken into, they saw their dog with the ass-end of a pair of jeans in his mouth and Smith's wallet in it — with his I.D. and everything else intact.

Ted went over and saw Smith, who hadn't had brains enough to change his pants. He was walking around the house in a pair of jeans with a big hole in them. Ted arrested him on the spot. Case closed.

• • •

Al returns for an encore:

The aforementioned Smith was such a rocket scientist that he once broke into a United Autoworkers' hall that was under construction. There was absolutely nothing in it to steal, but he broke in anyway. While there, he kicked over a bucket of white paint, strolled through the spilled stuff several times, and then walked down an alleyway to what he figured was freedom.

Police tracked his footprints down the alley and thence to a street near his home. Ho-hum, another case solved in a jiffy.

• • •

In February 1995 a Port Colborne, Ontario, armed bank robber made a rather unusual getaway, but thanks to a trio of helpful citizens, he was collared by the cops in jig time.

A man who claimed he had a gun demanded cash from a teller at a downtown bank. When he got the loot he rode off furiously through the snow — on a bicycle.

A bystander in the bank agreed to drive the manager to follow the robber, but they lost sight of him. Meanwhile, another eyewitness had also driven off to pursue the fleeing felon. A third man took off on foot to follow the crook's tracks in the snow.

A suspect was spotted at the back of a house. The citizen who was on foot stood watch while the driver of the second car drove back to the bank to relay the fugitive's location.

Police were called and they made the arrest within four minutes of the robbery. Money and a knife were seized by the arresting officers, and the culprit, who'd pulled other heists in the past, minus a bike, was shipped off to jail for five years.

• • •

Jim Ealey was a burglar no one could ever accuse of being bright.

One night in 1968, accompanied as usual by his dog, Jimmy knocked off a Detroit liquor store, then lugged home the loot as fast as he could. In his haste to vamoose, he neglected to notice he'd left the canine behind in the store.

When a police officer went to the scene of the crime he

shouted to the dog, "Home, boy!"

The policeman followed the pooch and promptly arrested his master.

• • •

A cheeky chap, arrested for an attempted break-in at a supermarket in Portsmouth, England, couldn't explain his highly suspicious actions to the judge — including why he was loitering in an alley as naked as the day he was born.

"The accused had been trying to get into the supermarket but couldn't squeeze through the skylight," said the Crown prosecutor. "He thought he'd be able to get in if he took his clothes off — and that's what he did. He pushed his clothes through the skylight, intending to follow them in, but to his dismay he still couldn't squeeze through. In desperation he shouted to a passing policeman, 'Get me out of here! I'm frozen!'"

The prisoner at the bar pleaded guilty to a charge of attempted breaking and entering.

"Yes, I had to shout to the copper for help," he told reporters later. "It was daft, but you see, lads, I'd been drinking a bit."

• • •

Constable Duncan Chisholm of the RCMP detachment in Deer Lake, Newfoundland, relates one of his all-time favourites about stupid crooks:

In Holyrood, Newfoundland, in 1984 I responded to a call from the proprietor of a well-known local business, who reported that the office safe had been sawed open and "all the money" taken away. When I arrived, the man who'd called said, "You won't believe this, officer. Just take a look at what's been done to this safe."

The door of the safe had been cut off completely and was lying on the floor a few feet away. I figured it must have taken the burglar about five hours to accomplish this feat.

"How much money did you lose?" I asked the owner.

"Two rolls of nickels and a roll of dimes," he replied.

I chuckled and said, "At last, I have an honest-to-God nickel-and-dime case."

"Well, hold it," the owner said. "It gets better — a lot better."

"What do you mean?" I asked eagerly.

"The safe wasn't even locked! We *never* lock it!"

• • •

A Florida bank robber ran from the scene of the crime clutching a sack of money and looking around anxiously for his buddy, the driver of the getaway car. He jumped into a vehicle of similar description, operated by a plainclothes policeman who, it just happened, was waiting for *his* sidekick at the time.

• • •

A young couple in Hoboken, New Jersey, pulled off a successful robbery, but failed miserably in their bid for a fast exit — they flagged down a police car they thought was a taxi and were driven straight to the slammer.

• • •

And in California in 1976 a chap named Alfred Rivera robbed a bar, then hotfooted it to a prearranged location where his accomplice waited anxiously for him to jump into the getaway car. A little too anxiously, it seems, for Al was run down by his overzealous partner, and the hapless pair were carted off to the clink.

• • •

In 1989 Anthony Colella robbed a bank in Brooklyn, New York, and escaped with $2,100. After he'd run about a block and a half, another man jumped out of a parked car, slugged him, and scampered off with the loot.

The outraged Colella trotted straight to the nearest police

station and reported the robbery. The police thanked him — and arrested him forthwith.

• • •

A British barrister, saddled with the hopeless task of defending a totally inept bank robber who'd been caught red-handed, tried gamely but vainly to convince the jury that there were some mitigating circumstances to be taken into account. Like, for instance, extreme stupidity.

"My client is basically innocent," he told the jurors. "Upon entering the bank that he later robbed, he got his foot caught in the revolving door and had to be helped to the counter by the lady he then threatened. On being told that the till did not contain the £5,000 he'd demanded, he reduced the ante, first to £500, then to £50, and finally to £5 and the offer of a drink around the corner."

• • •

Several years ago the San Diego Police Department's excellent but unfortunately now-defunct newsletter, *Up Front*, carried this cute little item under the heading "Dumb Criminal of the Month":

The prize goes to Roland Stewart, wanted for a Miami Beach homicide. Ol' Rollie was vacationing/hiding in San Diego when he called and turned himself in to SDPD Homicide. So far, so good? Wait for it.

Mr. Stewart turned himself in because he heard there was a $10,000 reward for his capture and he needed the money. Homicide detectives were heard muttering something about IQs below room temperature.

• • •

Up Front introduced another "Dumb Criminal of the Month" as follows:

El Cajon PD captured a purse-snatch suspect right after the fact and immediately set up a curbside ID. The police car drove the victim to the suspect's location, just like the directions said.

Before the astonished victim could get a word in, the crook peered into the police car and declared, "That's the lady I robbed — right there!"

The startled cop said, "Huh? Which one?" and the helpful robber clarified everything by saying, "The one in the pink."

Never forget, we catch only the DUMB ones.

• • •

In 1995 the Colorado Court of appeals dealt with a rather unappetizing case.

It all started when Filbert G. Maestas and an accomplice slipped into a meat-processing plant and swiped what they believed to be 1,200 juicy prime rib and T-bone steaks. But their haul consisted of the rectums of 1,200 butchered animals.

Maestas and friend were nabbed outside a meat warehouse by two policemen who found numerous cartons of this godawful cargo in their possession. When the warehouse manager was brought into the picture, he confirmed that the rectums, known in the beef business as rennets, had been stolen from the company plant.

As Maestas and his sidekick were being driven to the police station to be booked, one of the cops started to laugh. Maestas asked him what was so funny, and the officer told him that the rennets were inedible rectal tissue that could be used only in the curing of cheese.

Lapsing into plain lingo, the officer told the prisoners they'd stolen 1,200 assholes.

"If I go to jail for stealing 1,200 assholes, I'm really going to be mad," Maestas said in a highly serious tone.

The statement was used against him at his trial, and he and his accomplice were found guilty as charged. But Maestas

11

appealed to the Colorado Court of Appeals, claiming his remark was obtained illegally and saying he was thrown off guard because the policeman was laughing at him.

The panel of judges denied the appeal, stating that the officer had plenty of reason to be laughing.

• • •

A short, snappy news story published in 1995 read as follows:

VERNON, British Columbia — So just how stupid were the guys who tried to hold up a pharmacy in this Okanagan city the first week of January? Well, these two crooks must take first prize for the dumbest robbers of the year.

The RCMP say a man walked into the pharmacy January 4 and told an employee he was going to rob the place — and would be back in thirty minutes to do it.

Sure enough, the would-be crook and a buddy arrived half an hour later to carry out the robbery. The employee had called the RCMP, who were waiting with their long arms outstretched.

• • •

Stephen Saunders of Ottawa, Ontario, saw the humour in everything — including his collosal screwups as a criminal.

One memorable day in 1980 the twenty-four-year-old Saunders stole two cases of samples from a footwear salesman. Each case contained exactly one hundred left boots.

Weeks later Saunders swiped a chiropractor's business records and held them for ransom. But the note he left didn't say — or even hint — how much cash he wanted for their safe return.

Saunders was arrested after he picked up a phoney ransom packaged by police and left near his home by the chiropractor's receptionist.

But to his everlasting credit, the prisoner at the bar laughed heartily when he heard the facts of his fiascoes read aloud in open court.

• • •

Many robbers are just plain stupid when launching a crime and stay that way right up until their inevitable arrest. But it appears that some — a very small percentage, I'm sure — perform brilliantly for most of their felonious adventure and then suddenly become very, very stupid, indeed.

Take, for example, the imaginative big-league bank heist pulled in downtown Toronto on March 18, 1992, by a fearless rookie robber named Jack Santos.

The night before said caper Santos applied blond dye to his dark brown hair, hoping to disguise his appearance. Suddenly his locks were bright orange.

At noon the next day, Santos, posing as a policeman, was handed $3 million after showing a bank manager a gun (actually a broken air pistol) and some dynamite (actually Plasticine) wired around his waist. Santos crammed all the loot into a gym bag and left moments after telling the manager he'd planted a bomb on the premises — another tall tale, as it turned out. He then flagged down a taxi and headed home.

Experts agreed it was the perfect crime — until the robber recalled he'd left his apartment keys in an underground parking garage and decided to go back by cab to retrieve them. When he got to the garage, two blocks from the bank he'd knocked off, he decided he might as well drive home in his own vehicle. He ran smack-dab into a roadblock that had been put up to help nail a bandit with bright orange hair. The $3 million, every cent of it, was safe and sound in the gym bag on the back seat of the car.

Santos was convicted of bank robbery and handed a whopping seventeen-year jail sentence, which was later reduced to ten years by the Ontario Court of Appeal.

• • •

"The work of a criminal investigator is occasionally made a lot easier by the stupidity of the offenders," writes Jack Webster, former chief of the Metropolitan Toronto homicide squad, in his interesting autobiography, *Copper Jack*. He recalls a bank robber who left his hat at the scene of the crime, with his full name, including his middle initial, on the inside band. Finding and arresting this bozo was a snap.

But it's tough to top the case Webster now describes:

"During a large warehouse break and enter, in which $175,000 worth of television sets were stolen, one of the burglars was caught short, had a bowel movement, then wiped himself with his parole release form, which contained his name and address. I believe that the identification personnel on this occasion went above and beyond the call of duty when they delicately retrieved this important document and examined it."

• • •

Stuart Armstrong, of Oakville, Ontario, has many fond memories of humorous things that happened when he was a constable in Essex, England, from 1979 to 1981.

"One of them concerns an attempted bank robbery I helped investigate," he writes, and here is his tale:

A man entered a Lloyd's Bank with a handwritten note, which he gave to a teller. In the note he claimed to have a bomb, which he threatened to detonate if he wasn't given money.

The teller followed instructions and gave him cash. The crook then left the bank in such a hurry that he forgot to take the note with him. It was considerate of him to do this, because elsewhere on the paper the message was written on appeared his name and address. So we went around to his flat and caught him counting his spoils.

"I knew I'd forgotten something at the bank," he said pleasantly, "but damned if I could remember what it was."

• • •

In 1970 a biker bloke named Clive Bunyan made things rather easy for a copper who charged him with robbing the village store in Cayton, Yorkshire. While making the heist the culprit was wearing a crash helmet, across the front of which the words "CLIVE BUNYAN" appeared in large gold letters.

• • •

In Sarnia, Ontario, in July 1995 a bungling stickup man was sent to the clink for two years less a day when he pleaded guilty to robbing a bank of $2,000.

Before entering the bank this not-too-bright fellow ordered a taxi using his real name. Once in, he handed a teller a note demanding $50 and $100 bills or the bank would be blown up. But the note, which was written on a withdrawal slip, had his name and signature on it. As if all this weren't enough, he then told some "friends" about the heist and they ratted to the cops.

Oh, well, no one's perfect.

• • •

Anyone who runs afoul of the law would be extremely well advised to heed the words of the old saying, "He who acts as his own lawyer has a fool for a client."

Robert J. Lane, a lawyer in Shellbrook, Saskatchewan, provides proof positive that truer words were never spoken. Bob sent me a court-certified transcript of the arraignment, in Provincial Court in Prince Albert, of a fellow who represented himself on a charge of breaking and entering.

After the charge had been read to the accused, the court clerk informed him that he could elect to be tried in Provincial Court or in the Court of Queen's Bench, and then, for good measure, the judge explained the matter to him. This dialogue ensued:

JUDGE: Do you understand it now, or would you like further explanation?

ACCUSED: I understand it.

JUDGE: Do you feel that you're prepared to elect and plead today, or do you want me to adjourn so that you can take advice?

ACCUSED: I'll take it.

JUDGE: You want to elect today? Who do you elect?

ACCUSED: You.

JUDGE: And how do you plead, guilty or not guilty?

ACCUSED: I plead not guilty.

JUDGE (to the prosecutor): How many Crown witnesses will there be?

ACCUSED: Only one — the one I broke into the store with.

• • •

Constable George Cameron of the Summerside Police Department in Prince Edward Island wrote to me recently about a case he recalls that also confirms the aforementioned old saying:

An accused was charged with robbery and was brought before a judge to enter a plea. The accused, representing himself, was seated at the counsel table. The judge explained to the accused that he had the choice of being tried by a Provincial Court judge sitting alone, or by a Supreme Court judge and jury.

The judge then asked the accused, "How do you wish to be tried?"

The accused stood up, looked at the judge, and said, "Guilty, Your Honour."

• • •

A suspect in Tulsa, Oklahoma, defending himself on a purse-snatching charge, asked the victim on the witness stand, "Did you get a good look at me when I took your purse?"

• • •

In an Oregon case, a man who acted for himself in fighting a robbery charge asked the complainant on cross-examination, "Could you see my face clearly when I handed you the note?"

• • •

In Oklahoma City, a man handling his own defence in an armed-robbery case became angry when the victim identified him.

The defendant accused the witness of lying and screamed, "I should 'ave blown your head off!"

Then, realizing his error, he added quickly, but in vain, "if, that is, I'd been the one who was there."

• • •

Several years ago, in a California case, two men were on trial for armed robbery. An eyewitness took the stand, and while questioning him, the ever-so-careful prosecutor said, "So you say you were at the scene when the robbery took place?"

"Yes," replied the witness.

"And you saw a vehicle leave at a high rate of speed?"

"Yes."

"And did you observe the occupants?"

"Yes, two men."

"AND," boomed the prosecutor, "ARE THOSE TWO MEN PRESENT IN COURT TODAY?"

The defendants raised their hands and immediately sealed their fate.

• • •

In a recent Colorado robbery case, in which the identification of the culprits was the burning issue, one of the three accused men caused *his* part of the festivities to fizzle abruptly by saying, "The witness can't identify me because I had a mask on."

. . .

San Diego police were in hot pursuit of a man suspected of abducting a child. In rather short order they found the suspect's brother, who told them that the suspect was at their parents' house three blocks away. But the cops slipped up and let the brother leave. By the time they got to the parents' house, the brother they had talked to was already there.

The suspect was nowhere in sight, so police began a thorough search. They found their man hiding in a closet, frantically changing clothes in an attempt to disguise his identity. Upon seeing the officers, the fellow blurted out the following memorable message: "*I'm not me! I'm my brother!*"

. . .

An English judge who was rather hard of hearing presided at the trial of a man accused of a serious offence. The evidence against the accused was overwhelming, but he insisted on supplementing his counsel's speech with one of his own.

"I've never been in trouble before," the instant lawyer told the judge with considerable emotion, "and there are a number of matters that I feel I've got to clear up for the sake of my good reputation."

The accused spoke rapidly and excitedly, but he was understandable for the first few minutes of his address. Then he picked up speed, and from then on the judge had the devil of a time comprehending what he was saying. Finally, overcome by emotion and the novelty of his task, the chap became completely incoherent.

"Hold it!" said the judge, who'd been trying hard to jot down the main points of argument. "What was your last sentence?"

"Seven years," blurted the accused.

. . .

"Confession is good for the soul," goes the old expression.

Maybe, but it often louses up one's future.

In 1994 an Ontario fraud artist, who tried to steal more than $2.4 million, admitted in court that he wanted the money to finance a lifestyle of expensive cars, trips, jewellery, and gifts for friends. He pleaded guilty to seventeen charges of fraud and theft. More than $300,000 was not recovered.

He'd been caught because he'd stood in front of his church congregation during a special service and tearfully confessed his crimes, then begged the members to help him and his family. Instead, many of them called police.

"The phone kept ringing in our office," remarked a detective. "People from the congregation were lining up to turn him in, and in the end he was sentenced to a long stretch in prison."

● ● ●

A former policeman in Toronto, Ontario, told me this tale:

My partner and I were in a housing complex investigating a known drug dealer. During a consent search a large sum of cash — but no drugs — was found. We asked the suspect where he got the money, but he just said he found it.

We began looking through the cash, and my partner said, "Hey, look, this is the marked money that the drug squad used for its buys last week. This must be the wanted dealer."

I picked up my sidekick's little game, and I, too, looked at the money and agreed. "Yeah," I said, "this is definitely it."

The suspect started to look a little nervous, and I knew we had him. (Criminals are generally stupid.) He told us the money was for a charitable cause and said he didn't sell any drugs to undercover cops because he knew them all.

My partner said, "Well, if it's for charity, why don't we help you deliver it? It wouldn't be right if you got robbed."

We walked this guy right to the bank and watched him stuff all the cash in a box collecting money for a charity searching for bone-marrow donors for sick children. It may not have been by the book, but that drug money probably helped lots of kids.

• • •

Terry Cooper — not his real name — met Bob the Bug in a penitentiary in Springhill, Nova Scotia, back in the 1980s, when both were serving terms of several years' duration. Terry's on the "outside" now and has a business that's starting to flourish. He says that Bob, an incredibly inept crook, is probably in the pen, or will be returning there soon, because "he always comes back."

I asked Terry why his old pal is called Bob the Bug. "Does it mean he bugs people?" I wondered.

"No," Terry replied. "A bug, in prison lingo, is an inmate who's very bright and does offbeat things, is a nonconformist and a loner, minds his own business and has few good friends, doesn't join organizations or cliques, makes elaborate plans that often lead to calamitous results — that sort of guy."

Terry tells us about the night Bob and a couple of his confederates decided to rob a sporting-goods store, steal a bunch of guns, and then sell them to buy drugs:

First, they stole a large van and actually pulled off the late-night break and enter without incident. The three of them were stoned on weed while driving out of town, and they soon noticed a cop on their tail. Ahead of them was a hitchhiker.

To see if the cop was following them or not, they stopped and picked this guy up. The cop pulled over, too, about a hundred yards behind them. This spooked the driver and he raced away just as the hitchhiker made it into the van. The hitchhiker saw all the guns that were spread over the floor of the van and he started freaking out. He said he wanted to get out of the vehicle right then and there.

This set off the three crooks, and Bob overreacted. He

assembled one of the shotguns, loaded it, and fired through the back window at the cop car. The blast scared his unprepared driver, and he lost control of the van. The vehicle left the road and hit a tree. All three went directly to jail with no one hurt.

• • •

Sometimes Bob the Bug flew solo:

Bob cased a drugstore he was interested in, and noticed a good alarm system and a fridge in the dispensary that was full of fun drugs. He counted the twelve-inch-square floor tiles from the left to the fridge and from the storefront to the fridge, so he could measure that off from the basement.

On a Saturday night he broke into the place next door, went to the basement, sledgehammered a hole through the wall, and soon he was under the drugstore. He measured off the distances to locate the fridge above and marked it out on the basement ceiling. Then he fired up his chain saw and shoved the cutting bar right up through the floor to make the first cut.

Bob got a three-sided cut done that resembled a square with one of the vertical lines missing, and before he could get out of the way the floor buckled and down came the fridge — right on top of him! That's where they found him Monday morning.

So it was back to the slammer for Bob the Bug.

• • •

Some of Bob's adventures were downright farcical. Terry describes two such episodes:

The drugstore caper got Bob a term at Dorchester Penitentiary in New Brunswick, where he made inmate workclothes for a "living." These clothes got shipped to other prisons in six-by-six-foot crates. One Friday afternoon, Bob packed himself into a crate on the loading dock and waited for the truck that was scheduled to come for the pickup.

Unfortunately the forklift operator put another crate on top of the one Bob was in *and* the truck didn't arrive. The truck didn't show up because at the 4:00 p.m. headcount the guards were one body short — Bob the Bug's body — and the joint was locked up tight with no in or out traffic permitted.

Bob spent the weekend in the crate, in the sun, on the dock. He was calling for help by Monday morning. Off to a medium-security joint after the stunt at the minimum-security Dorchester.

By now Bob was thirty-three and he had spent seventeen years locked up in one institution or another slightly more than half his life — all for stupid shit like this. He finally made day parole and decided to break into the premises of a large drug-manufacturing company for the big score he hoped would allow him to retire with lots and lots of dough at his disposal.

He figured that, due to the high-tech security system that was in place, his best way into the building was through the air conditioner on the roof. He eventually wriggled himself into the three-by-four-foot sheet-metal duct feeding the interior. He was on his back, doing a feet-first crawl, looking down vents and to his left and right, trying to figure out where the hell he was, lost in the maze of duct work.

Claustrophobia soon kicked in and he started to panic, now hopelessly lost in the ducts. His kicking and thrashing tore one of the support straps loose, and the duct work fell about six feet before bending in a forty-five-degree shape that looked like a V. Bob was in the bottom of that V when they found him in the morning.

• • •

With narrator Terry Cooper still at the helm, we now sail off to the bounding main:

Nova Scotia is a drug smuggler's heaven. There are thousands of deep inlets all along the 4,625-mile coastline of the province. Buy a fishing boat, pick up the drugs from the mother ship posing as a trawler off the Grand Banks, take it to the dropoff inlet and unload. Then take the boat out to deep water and blow it up or sink it — there's no evidence that a crime was ever committed.

On the chance that you might get caught on the way back (local fishermen watch for such activity and some report it), the bags of dope get weighted down with rock salt so they'll sink. If you see someone following you, chuck the dope overboard — it sinks, the salt dissolves, and the bags pop up again in eight to ten hours. That's how it's *supposed* to go.

These two city boys from Ontario followed these steps to a T, except for the salt. It was winter, so the chemical stuff you use on driveways and such was readily available and cheap. I don't know what it's made of, but it's not salt! It's calcium chloride something-or-other, and it even keeps slush from refreezing after it's melted the ice. When this stuff hits water it goes off like the old dry-ice-in-the-toilet trick — BOOM!!!

To make a long story short, the Ontario guys got caught. When the jettisoned bags hit the water they *didn't* sink, but each one of them zoomed off, shooting around on the surface of the water like forty little "seadoos." They were making such weird patterns on a Coast Guard radar screen that someone went out to investigate.

Seven years for each for importation of drugs.

2

WHEELS

Everything in life is somewhere else,
and you get there in a car.
— E.B. White

Except for three stories about trains and motorcycles and one pertaining to a driver's test, this chapter is all about cars — police cars and private cars and the endless ways their drivers manage to get into trouble. So hop in, buckle your seat belts, and we'll get this crazy show on the road.

Because they deal with so many lippy motorists, I'm sure countless cops around the world will appreciate the following little exchange, submitted by an anonymous member of the Edmonton, Alberta, police force:

One of our officers stopped a motorist and asked to see his driver's licence. The man went into a huff and demanded to know why the policeman wanted to see it.

"Because you were driving," the constable said sweetly. "If you were fishing, I'd ask to see your fishing licence."

• • •

And, speaking of said subject and said city . . .

One day in 1980 an Edmonton cop who was about to go off duty gave a speeding ticket to a man who hailed from Virginia. The officer, perhaps preoccupied with pending events, wrote on the ticket — twice, yet! — that the offender lived at a certain address in "Arlington, Vagina."

• • •

Police Officer Kirk J. Roncskevitz of Nashville, Tennessee, believes it isn't always true that "a rose by any other name would smell as sweet." He tells us about a scary close call he had one day while questioning a woman he'd stopped for a traffic violation:

As was my habit, I intended to address her as "Ms." and then add her last name, but I came to a screeching halt on the last name — Fux. Having excellent training and experience thinking on my feet in tense and dangerous situations, at the last split second I said, "Fooks."

• • •

Constable Mark Tregellas, of Portland, Victoria, Australia, files this report on a Yuletide wager:

One Christmas Eve in Portland I was driving a police cruiser when I spotted a cyclist — with no lights or helmet — flying down a street. We took off after him and saw him turn right into a street, where he dumped the bike in some bushes and started walking back towards the street corner. We pulled up next to him and had the following conversation:

ME: G'day, matey, what are you up to?
HIM: Waitin' for a taxi.
ME: I beg your pardon?
HIM: Waitin' for a taxi.
ME: And where did you call the taxi from? Your bike phone?
HIM: No, the pub.
ME: What pub?
HIM: The Royal (a pub about a kilometre from where we were).
ME: You called a taxi from the Royal and told it to meet you down here?
HIM: Yes.
ME: That's the biggest load of rubbish I've ever heard. I wasn't going to book anyone tonight, but in your case I'll make an exception.

As I started filling out a penalty notice, the sergeant who was travelling with me leaned over and asked a couple of questions.

SERGEANT: So what you're saying is, if we wait here for five minutes a taxi will show up?
HIM: Yes.
SERGEANT: Sport, if a taxi shows up in the next two minutes, I'll pay your fare.
HIM: Okay.

As I finished writing out the penalty notice and handed it to the bloke, a taxi came around the corner and stopped. The driver leaned out of the window and said, "You ready, mate?"

I felt pretty small, but the sergeant felt smaller. And so did his wallet.

• • •

John Golightly, of Kincardineshire, Scotland, has a lighthearted tale about an incident that occurred when his son Stephen was a junior constable in nearby Grampian:

Whilst Stephen was accompanying his tutor constable in a
patrol car one evening in Banff, they spotted some youths carrying on in the road ahead. The youngsters had spilled out onto
the pavement after a discotheque had closed. One of them was
obviously the worst for drink, and was singing and waving his
arms madly.

The tutor said to my son, "Right, we'll hae him the nicht!"

Stopping the car alongside the youth, the constable noticed
on the other side of the road another two youths carrying on. He
wound down his window and bellowed at them, "Hey, keep the
noise doon or you'll be spending the nicht in the cells!"

He then focused his attention on the original youth, who at
this time was banging on the bonnet of the patrol car, waving his
hands and loudly using foul language directed at the officers.

This apparent disrespect for the police infuriated the tutor
constable, who turned to my son and said, "Right, we'll definitely hae him," and then inquired as to what my son, who was
now in stitches, found so funny.

My son laughingly replied, "You've stopped the car on his
foot!"

• • •

Donatas Z. Cernius, of London, Ontario, recently retired from
the Ontario Provincial Police after thirty years of service. He
wrote to me about a memorable traffic case he once had that
went from bad to verse:

Back in 1964, when I was a young OPP traffic officer patrolling
the Queen Elizabeth Way in the Burlington area, I observed a
car being driven erratically. As I caught up with the offending
vehicle, I noticed that the oldish gent driving was having a
hard time seeing through a dirty windshield. The wipers were

operational but were useless for want of windshield fluid. So I wrote him up and we parted company.

As it turned out, the gentleman, Norman St. Croix of Hamilton, Ontario, sent in his fine, as well as a poem he'd written about the "bust," to the courthouse in Oakville. Someone there sent a copy of the poem to me. Alas, Ma Bell has no listing for this poet, and I fear he may no longer be with us.

The following is the accused's lyrical lament:

For the Defence

One early Sunday morning,
While the Queen E. I was driving,
Came a violent, horn-blown warning
That a police car was arriving.
And my trusty rearview mirror
Told me clearly that a "Copper"
Was to fill my life with terror,
If my car I didn't stop 'er.

So I pulled far off the highway,
And I waited for his Highness,
Who (belligerent) came my way
And inquired of my "dryness."
"Are you drunk?" I quote him saying,
"No, No, No," I kept replying,
(While admitting I was praying,
That he couldn't prove me lying.)

"What great crime have I committed?"
Said I to this law enforcer;
(While admitting I'm dim-witted,
I admit to nothing worser.)
"You are driving quite erratic,"
Said this Gendarme, rather grimly,

Which, of course, made me ecstatic,
Since I viewed his viewpoint dimly.

"You are charged," he said, "with driving
While your windshield is obstructed.
You can see that I am striving
In my duty — as instructed."

Well, I couldn't help but wonder
How I'd driven far — from Toronto —
Without any sign of blunder,
Until up beside me — pronto —
Came this angel out of nowhere,
Doing, what he thought, his duties,
As I stood there, on the snow, there,
Eyes downcast toward his bootees.

So, dear Judge, though I plead, clearly,
That I follow no religion,
And, for sin, I must pay dearly,
Like a sitting duck or pigeon.
Let's congratulate the "Copper"
Who is, more or less, efficient,
And brings those of us a cropper
Whom (he judges) drive deficient.

For the law, Sir, I respect, Sir,
Like a man respects his mother;
If I break it, I expect, Sir,
To pay up — like any other.
So enclosed, please find your fine, Sir,
And accept my plea, so humble,
That my driving did decline, Sir —
And my faith in Justice crumble!

• • •

Lewis Howells, of Pontllanfraith, Gwent, Wales, sent me an auto-motive tale from yesteryear. It was told to him by a friend of his who was the policeman in question:

When motorcars were few and far between and scarcely out on the road, the appearance of a strange vehicle in the countryside would arouse suspicions and trigger off a kind of "neighbour-hood watch" reaction.

A farmer observed a strange vehicle parked for a considerable length of time in a little-used country lane on several consecutive Wednesdays. The farmer decided to contact the local policeman and ask him to go along to this lane to have a look, if it wasn't too much trouble. Working amicably and closely with the rural community, the policeman readily agreed and went to investigate this strange car parked in the quiet country lane.

He arrived to find a man and woman revelling in the fullest joys of lovemaking. Whereas nowadays a broader, more toler-ant attitude might be exercised towards this sort of activity taking place in a remote spot, at that time a sterner approach had to be taken by the law.

The policeman tapped on the car and called on the occupants to stop and get dressed, and he told them that he would return to have a few words with them after discreetly retreating for a while. Upon his return, he was somewhat surprised to learn that the man was, in fact, a man of the cloth!

Straight to the point, the policeman's opening remarks were to the effect that this car had been observed parked in the same place in the lane on the previous Wednesday, and on other Wednesdays before that, and that this behaviour had to stop.

Quick as a flash the woman piped up, "Oh, it wasn't us! We weren't here last Wednesday!"

But the clergyman remained shiftily silent.

• • •

On a bitterly cold winter day in northern British Columbia, a Royal Canadian Mounted Police constable on patrol came across a motorcyclist, swathed in protective clothing and helmet, stalled by the roadside.

"What's the matter?" asked the officer.

"Carburetor's frozen."

"Just piss on it. That'll thaw it out."

"I can't."

"Okay, I will."

The Mountie undid his fly and peed all over the curburetor. The bike started up again and the rider waved and rode off.

A few days later, the RCMP detachment office received a note of thanks from the father of the motorcyclist. It began:

"On behalf of my daughter, who recently was stranded . . ."

• • •

One evening a few years back a couple of police officers patrolling a highway in England noticed a snazzy Rolls-Royce parked on the shoulder of the road and a man standing beside the car having a long, pleasurable pee. The patrol car stopped and one of the officers asked the bloke, "What are you doing?"

"The answer should be obvious," the man replied as he tucked his member back into its usual resting place. "I was short-taken, and since there was virtually no traffic on the road I took a chance and relieved myself beside the car."

The policeman then asked him if he'd been drinking, and when the man said he had he was given a roadside Breathalyzer test, which he flunked badly.

It was decided that one of the officers would drive to police headquarters in the the patrol car and his sidekick would deliver the tipsy citizen to jail in the Rolls. Only when his partner had left and he'd walked up to the driver's door did the other copper

31

see the chauffeur, who'd been waiting patiently — and soberly — for his boss to return to the car.

• • •

A policeman patrolling a highway in Oxfordshire, England, was alarmed to see a naked woman leaning out the window of a passing car and apparently waving for help. He gave chase and soon stopped the other vehicle.

It turned out the damsel in distress was in fact a life-size inflatable doll with — as the cop later testified — "breasts and other convincing attributes."

The driver told the cop his wife had recently deserted him and the doll was a gift from friends who were trying to cheer him up.

"After a few drinks I took a liking to the doll," the man confessed, "and I decided to take her for a spin in the country."

The officer wasn't convinced — nor were the magistrates, who fined the fellow £25 for "carrying a dangerous load."

• • •

There's nothing inherently funny about drinking and driving, what with all the injuries, deaths, and destruction that can result. But laughter lurks everywhere, and every now and then it crops up in the course of a drinking-and-driving investigation.

Just ask Carl Crider, a policeman in the Dallas, Texas, suburb of Garland. Crider was absolutely astonished by something he saw one memorable day in 1961.

The tipsy driver he was chasing wheeled into a driveway in a residential area and drove right into the garage. Crider parked his cruiser and walked into the garage to meet the motorist.

"Let me see your driver's licence," he told the man.

"I'm on my own property," the fellow snapped, "and I'm going to go in right now and hit the sack."

Crider knew it was a bluff . . . and called it.

"Not in my house, you're not," he said quietly.

• • •

A few years ago, Judge Harold Gyles of Winnipeg, Manitoba, reminisced with me about the "bad old days," before Breathalyzer tests were made mandatory in cases of suspected impaired driving.

"Back then," he said, "the suspect practically had to be holding on to the grass so he wouldn't roll off the world before he could be convicted of driving while impaired by alcohol."

His Honour told me about a case in which an RCMP officer testified that he stopped a motorist after seeing his car weaving over the centre line of the highway. The driver lowered his window and the officer said, "Let me see your driver's licence."

The man dropped his wallet on the floor of the car, fumbled for it, found it after a great deal of groping, and then extracted a card for the policeman.

The officer stared at it, puzzled.

"Why, when I asked for your driver's licence, have you given me your Manitoba medical card?" he inquired.

"Because," said the fast-thinking suspect, "I thought I'd give you something to read while I looked for my licence."

• • •

In another drinking-and-driving case before Breathalyzer tests were mandatory, Judge Gyles said that a Brandon, Manitoba, man was, in effect, rewarded for his sense of humour.

A policeman saw this fellow lose control of his car, drive over the median, and then, amazingly, negotiate a slalom course through a grove of trees, without even nicking one of them.

"Have you been drinking?" the officer asked when he caught up with the motorist.

"Of course I've been drinking," the man replied. "What do you think I am, a stunt driver?"

The cop laughed so hard he didn't lay a charge.

• • •

In a case in Astoria, Oregon, the defendant, an elderly woman, steadfastly insisted she wasn't guilty of drunk driving. Here's part of the prosecutor's examination of the arresting officer:

Q. Now, Officer, where was the defendant when you first encountered her?

A. She was still in her car with the motor running, and the car was off the road and straddling a large log with all four wheels off the ground and spinning.

Q. And what was it about this incident that led you to suspect that the defendant was intoxicated?

A. I climbed on the log and knocked on her window, which was closed. She rolled the window down and gave me a strange look, then looked at her speedometer. Then she looked up and said, "How can you be keeping up with me? I'm doing forty miles an hour."

A lawyer reports that the defendant changed her plea "immediately after this testimony."

• • •

If they don't want suspects foiling them left and right, cops have to be quick-witted and resourceful; at times, exceedingly so. Such a person is Sergeant Jim Liles, a nineteen-year veteran of the Covington Police Department in Kentucky.

One night when Liles had been on the force only three years, he learned a lot about resourcefulness, and it's stood him in good stead ever since. About 2:00 a.m. that memorable night he stopped a car he'd seen weaving all over the road and approached the driver, a sixty-plus, six-foot-three, 240-pound man we'll call George, who displayed all the usual signs of impairment and flunked several sobriety tests, to boot:

I arrested George for driving under the influence and told him to put his hands behind his back to be handcuffed. I grabbed his arm to cuff him, and he tried to struggle and break free. I pushed him to the trunk area of my cruiser and got his hands behind his back and handcuffed. I put him in the back of the car, and he started yelling that he'd been in the Marines and he'd never been treated like this.

After I arranged for his car to be towed, I drove him to the jail, where he refused to get out of the cruiser. I told him if he didn't get out I'd drag him out. He refused several more times, stating he'd been a sergeant in the Marine Corps and had never been treated like this. I called to have the jail send someone out to help me get George out of the car and for a wheelchair to sit him in. A jailer brought a grocery cart. He couldn't get George in that, so again I asked George to leave my cruiser. He refused, so I hauled him out onto the ground. He refused to get up and I could see some cuts on his wrist from the cuffs. I was so mad I just walked away from George, who was still on the ground yelling about being in the Marines and being treated so bad.

I then took my hat off, walked around my cruiser to the other side of George, and yelled, "Sergeant George, this is Captain Liles, Third Marine Division! What have these people done to you? Get on your feet, Sergeant, and let me take those cuffs off!"

George looked at me and said, "Yes, sir, Captain!" He got up and I took the cuffs off him, at which time George clicked his heels, saluted me, and said, "Thank you, Captain!" I told George to follow me, and he saluted me again and stated, "I will follow you anywhere, Captain!"

I walked George into the police department, which was on the second floor of the county building. I had asked him earlier to take a Breathalyzer test, and he had refused. In my new role as an officer in the Marines, I asked him once again to take such a test. He declared, "I will do anything you ask, Captain." He took the Breathalyzer test and then I marched him to the booking desk.

I was five foot ten, 185 pounds, with dark, medium-length

hair and no moustache. The officer behind the booking desk was five foot six, 150 pounds, balding, had a moustache, and wore glasses. I looked at George and said, "Isn't that the officer who arrested you and treated you so badly?" George started cussing and yelling at that officer and saying, "That's him, all right, that SOB!"

I then shouted, "Sergeant George, ATTENTION!" He clicked his heels, saluted me, and said, "Yes,*sir!*" I said, "Follow me, Sergeant." George saluted me again and stated, "Captain, I will follow you anywhere." I lodged George in the jail on the tenth floor. As I was leaving and the elevator door closed, George saluted me once again, for old time's sake, I guess, and concluded with a rousing, "Thank you, Captain!"

• • •

The Martians have landed! The Martians have landed!

On the last night of May 1985, two men we'll call Jones and Smith drove a truck through the Ontario counties of Huron and Bruce, stopping frequently for fresh transfusions of grog. It was a night to remember — if only they could. These fellows were plastered.

At about 3:30 a.m., near the village of Formosa, Jones braked and stopped the truck behind a van that was parked on the shoulder of the road. Smith was asleep in the passenger seat.

Jones scrambled out of his vehicle and staggered up to the van. He rapped on the window and woke the sole occupant, a man named Panayote Alafoyannis. Startled, Alafoyannis opened the door slightly and peered into the inky night.

"What are you doing here?" roared Jones.

Alafoyannis didn't answer. "I locked the door," he later told police. "The man punched the window and yelled, 'Come on outside and I'll kill you!' Then he started rocking the van."

After a while Jones left, got into his truck, and backed it into a ditch.

"I saw him and another guy walk to a farmhouse," Alafoyannis said. "They came back and the other guy got back into the truck. Then the first guy came back to my van again and started hollering, 'Come out and I'll kill you!'"

Alafoyannis had had enough. He honked his horn several times, and a few seconds later two dozen strange-looking little men came running through the darkness, heading for the van.

Jones gulped when he got a good look at the apparitions that milled around him. They were all about five feet tall and wore metal hats with lights on them. Aprons with big pockets covered their legs, and bulky baskets hung from their necks.

"Martians!" Jones screamed as he ran through the thicket of bobbing lights.

A few minutes later, Jones pounded on the door of a farmhouse, shouting all the while that Martians were in the neighbourhood.

Before the man of the house could make it to the door, Jones lurched over to a nearby station wagon, the key of which was in the ignition. The man arrived at the door just in time to see his wife's car speeding down the laneway. He called the Ontario Provincial Police in Walkerton, about seven miles to the east, and reported what had happened.

OPP constables Kevin Washnuk and John Potts had just driven out of their detachment when they spotted the station wagon that had been reported stolen a few minutes earlier. They did a quick U-turn, caught up with Jones, and stopped him. Jones staggered when he got out of the vehicle.

"Thank God you're here!" he said excitedly. "I was just coming to get you! You won't *believe* what happened! The Martians have landed and you gotta *do* something!"

"You bet," the cops said as they booked Jones for car theft.

"No, guys, I really saw Martians — little wee fellows with lights on their foreheads! They're kicking the shit outta my buddy, and I just had to get here so you'd know what happened

37

and you could go out there and *do* something about it!"

The police officers told Jones he was also charged with impaired driving, and they demanded a breath sample. He refused and was slapped with yet another charge.

At about 4:40 a.m., constables Washnuk and Potts found Jones's pickup in the ditch. Smith was sprawled across the front seat, still asleep. The officers questioned him, and it was apparent that he'd missed the entire "invasion."

A few minutes later the officers noticed numerous lights in a nearby field. They got up close and saw, in Washnuk's words, "two dozen men, all about five feet tall, some on their knees, some squatting, some crouched over." They wore metal hats with lights in the front, Washnuk said, and they wore "slimy, dirty aprons" and had baskets hanging from their necks.

So Jones was right, right? These fellows really were Martians, right?

Wrong!

They were Japanese-Canadian worm-pickers, up from Toronto, pulling in a commercial catch.

None of them could speak English, so the police weren't able to worm anything out of them. But they got a statement from foreman Alafoyannis, and when Crown attorney Brian Farmer learned the whole story he agreed with defence counsel Jim Donnelly that Jones, in his drunken state, honestly believed he was up to his arse in Martians and *had* to swipe the car to flee to safety. So the theft charge was dropped and Jones pleaded guilty to impaired driving and refusing to provide a breath sample.

• • •

Sergeant Gary Dale of Port Elgin, Ontario, has been a police officer for twenty-three years. Of all the hundreds of cases he's handled in that time, the one that never fails to convulse him is an impaired-driving investigation he conducted in the summer of 1979 when he was a constable in the nearby town of Hanover.

It was a spectacular show, and he now gleefully slips us all the sordid details.

The Drunk Driver Who Lost Control

I was working the midnight shift and all was quiet. At about 3:30 a.m. I was patrolling in my cruiser when I saw a car travelling at a very high rate of speed. A man was behind the wheel and he had a female passenger. I got in behind this car and activated my rooftop lights. The driver increased his speed. I then turned on the siren, but that didn't stop the car, either. Finally the man parked his vehicle under a streetlight in a residential area of town, and I left the cruiser and walked towards it. The man and woman got out of the vehicle, and as soon as I saw them I recognized them as Jim and Judy Johnson (not their real names), a couple I knew quite well.

Neither of these folks was feeling any pain, especially Jim. He had a strong odour of an alcoholic beverage on his breath, he was very unsteady on his feet, he had poor coordination, his eyes were bloodshot, and his speech was slurred — all the classic symptoms of impairment.

Up till then it was just a simple case of impaired driving. The problem was that I knew both of these people well, but I still had to do my job. Standing in the darkness, roof lights of the cruiser still spinning, flooding the neighbourhood with flashing red light, I took hold of Jim's arm and placed him under arrest.

Now the excitement really began. Judy started urging me not to arrest her husband. "Aw, come on, Gary," she said, "we were at a party. You don't have to do this. Gary, please, I'm begging you!"

At this point, as I stood beside Jim, I detected another strong odour — this one of human excrement. I continued the arrest ritual, advising Jim of his rights and reading a demand for breath samples, while Judy kept pleading her husband's case.

I continued to smell this odour, and after I'd read the breath demand Jim promptly told me that he couldn't go with me. I asked why and he replied, half moaning and half crying, *"Because I shit myself, Gary!"*

I had just asked Jim to take a seat in the cruiser when he quickly unfastened his belt and trousers and let his drawers drop to the ground. To my shock and dismay, there Jim stood, pants around his ankles — and he had obviously been telling the truth.

Now Jim decided he was going to get into my cruiser in this state! I quickly interceded and stopped him from doing so. The three of us were standing by the back of the cruiser on a quiet street. I was trying to decide what to do with him, and while Judy bleated on about the injustice of it all, Jim kicked off his pants completely. There he was, standing in the middle of the lighted intersection, naked from the waist down. Jim continued to tell me he wouldn't come with me for breath tests, and while removing his shirt he started walking towards his home two blocks away. Judy picked up her husband's clothes and staggered off into the darkness.

I secured their vehicle, then returned to the station to write reports. About 6:00 a.m. I received a call from Judy Johnson, who reported in a drunken slur that her husband hadn't returned home yet. This meant that Jim was walking around the neighbourhood naked from the waist down, and it was almost daylight.

I drove over to their neighbourhood and searched the area but couldn't see him anywhere. I then went to the Johnson residence and took a statement from Judy. She was worried that Jim might have had a heart attack, and I was worried about other things, such as a naked adult tromping through people's yards and sending the people into a panic.

As I was taking down details about Jim, Judy and I heard a loud splash in their swimming pool, followed almost immediately by a slurred voice shouting, *"Bring me a beer!"* I looked at Judy and said, "I think Jim's home," and then got up and left. Jim later attended at court and sheepishly pleaded guilty to charges of impaired driving and refusing to give a breath sample.

A few neighbours had stepped outside their doors to see what the commotion was all about, including a former policeman and his wife who laughed hysterically throughout the strip show, which they watched from behind a hedge. The husband told me it was the funniest thing he'd ever seen. And, coming from an ex-cop, that's high praise, indeed.

• • •

Some people simply don't have the brains to drive a car. Thank heavens for testing, as this story from Sergeant Denis M. Stanes, of Korumburra, Victoria, Australia, makes crystal clear. It happened one memorable morning in 1981 when a would-be driver came to the police station to crack off a simple test for his learner's permit.

What a Bloody Test!

It was a written test of thirty-two questions with multichoice answers, and all the applicant had to do was tick the right box. If anyone got more than four questions wrong or took longer than twenty minutes to finish the test, we were required to fail the applicant and tell him or her to try again later.

I arrived a few minutes after 9:00 a.m. that day. A young lady named Kerry and a chap named Robert Brown had just started their learner's-permit test. By 9:10, Kerry was finished. I corrected her test using a plastic "lay over" correction sheet, which had squares printed on it where the correct answer appeared on the test paper. Kerry passed, and after giving her an eye test and colour test, I filled out the permit application and collected the fee. She was gone by 9:20.

At this time Brown was still doing his test. At 9:30, the next applicant arrived and started in on her test. Seven or eight minutes later, the young lass was up at the counter, having finished her test, and I corrected it, using the same method. Then came the eye test, the colour test, the completion of the permit application and the collecting of the fee, and she was gone by 9:45.

But Brown was still sitting there, and I was concerned.

"Have you nearly finished?" I asked him.

"Yes," he replied, "I've only got two questions to go."

Six minutes later he said he'd finished, then added, "Gee, that was a hard test!"

I laid the form out, looking at the test-paper number on the reverse side, which in this case was thirty-two. I then took the appropriate plastic lay over and placed it on top of his test paper. Looking down the columns to see how many he had got wrong, I checked and checked again and, to my amazement, *I could not find one correct answer*!

Thinking I had done something wrong, I turned the plastic lay over a number of ways — and still I could not find any correct answers. At this stage I was thinking, How can anyone get *all* thirty-two questions wrong? Surely he'd get at least one or two of them right. I wondered how in hell I was going to break the news to him.

I said, "Gosh, Mr. Brown, you didn't do too well. I can't find one correct answer."

He was flabbergasted. Then he said, "Well, it was a very hard test, you know."

"What was so hard about it?" I inquired.

"Well, I couldn't even understand any of the questions."

"What do you mean?" I asked.

"Well," he said, "see if *you* can read it."

I looked down at the test paper and was amazed to see that it was printed entirely in *Italian*! I looked back up at Brown and started laughing.

"You've got to be joking," I said.

"What do you mean?"

"I mean, you've been sitting there for fifty minutes trying to read this?" I asked in wonderment. "Why didn't you *say* something?"

"Well," Brown said, "I thought that was part of the test — you know, trying to guess what the words meant."

I asked who gave him the test paper, and he said it was the senior sergeant.

I hotfooted it into the senior sergeant's office with the test paper and in a voice of sheer amazement asked, "Did you give this test paper to the bloke out there?"

"The young bloke who came in at 9:00 a.m.?" my boss inquired.

"Yes," I said, and told him what had happened. We both roared with laughter and Brown just couldn't see what was funny about any of this.

I then gave Brown a learner's-permit test in English, which was completed quite a bit faster than the one in Italian.

After correcting it I didn't feel quite so bad, as this time he only got *four* of the questions right!

• • •

A few years ago, an Edmonton policeman stopped a motorist he suspected of being impaired. The officer decided to conduct a sobriety test on the man and asked him to read a nearby sign.

"Before you start, do you normally wear glasses?" he asked the suspect.

"No, but I have contacts," the man replied.

Suddenly the policeman became flustered and snapped, "I don't care who you know. Just read the sign!"

• • •

Garney Arcand, deputy chief of police in Bellevue, Washington, sent me this speeding story that's well-known in his neck of the woods:

Many years ago in our city a woman was driving down the street, paying little attention to her speedometer, when she was startled by the sound of a siren and the sight of a marked patrol

43

car behind her. As the police officer approached her car, she was very flustered and was frantically trying to think of something to say to him when he got to her window.

Before he could say a word, she blurted, "I know — you stopped me to sell me tickets to the Policemen's Ball."

The officer looked down at the woman and stated seriously, "Lady, Bellevue policemen don't have balls."

• • •

An Edmonton, Alberta, policeman relates this little tale:

One of our traffic officers stopped a violator at a radar site. The motorist questioned the accuracy of radar, saying he'd read an article that indicated that a tree in Florida had been clocked at sixty miles an hour. The officer replied, "We don't have that problem here. Alberta trees can't go that fast."

• • •

St. John's, Newfoundland, lawyer and former policeman, Michael J. Laurie, reports that one day back in 1974 he was in court in Harbour Grace when a young fellow was charged with speeding. The case was disposed of swiftly and without any reference to radar.

The Crown offered only the evidence of two old-timers from the nearby fishing settlement of Upper Island Cove, who witnessed the youth's driving.

Michael says he'll never forget the terse testimony that scuppered the prisoner at the bar and set him back a cool ten bucks.

"Asked by the policeman-prosecutor how he knew the accused was speeding," he writes, "one old fisherman, in his lilting West Country dialect, barely akin to North American English, said in his sing-songy voice, 'Yar Hona, hi sed to me buddy, 'ayre 'e kums! 'n 'e sed, 'dar 'e goes!'"

• • •

Lieutenant Roger A. Gross of the United States Park Police in Washington, D.C., narrates this amusing example of justice Southern-style:

When I went to Washington for my formal swearing-in with the United States Park Police, I was told that one of the United States magistrates in Maryland was an ex-FBI agent who had obtained his law degree and was very pro-police.

The U.S. Park Police have authority in all national parks in the United States, but mostly work in the Washington, D.C., metropolitan area, Gateway National Recreation Area, and Golden Gate National Recreation Area. In the D.C. area, the Park Police patrol the Baltimore-Washington (B.W.) Parkway. The B.W. is a north-south corridor linking Washington with Baltimore and points north.

The United States magistrates are empowered to handle violations of state motor-vehicle traffic laws. Many northern travellers have had to face the wrath of Southern justice.

One evening, a motorist from the New York City area was driving south on the B.W. when he was picked up on radar going at an excessive speed. He was pulled over and asked to follow the officer to the U.S. magistrate's office, which was in the magistrate's home. The officer brought the driver into the hearing room and told the magistrate what the charge was.

The driver, when asked if he had anything to say, stated with some arrogance and annoyance, "I'm in a rush. What's the fine?"

The magistrate replied, "Fifty dollars."

The driver stated in the same arrogant tone of voice, "I can pay that!" He reached into his pocket and pulled out a large wad of cash. He peeled off the fine and slapped it onto the desk in the hearing room, then put the wad back into his pocket.

Annoyed by the man's arrogance, the magistrate said,

"That's contempt of court. That'll cost you another fifty dollars."

The driver was not slowed down by the contempt ruling and stated, "No problem, I can pay that, too!"

He reached into his pocket and peeled off another fifty dollars and tossed it on the hearing-room desk.

Outraged that the driver would throw the second fine on the desk after being cited for contempt, the magistrate told him, "Now reach into your other pocket and pull out thirty days!"

The magistrate had the man removed to the local lockup where he got a chance to ponder the justice sometimes meted out south of the Mason-Dixon Line.

• • •

"It's interesting, the effect police have on people," Detective Terry L. Davis, of Lemoore, California, wrote in a letter to me. He shared this funny anecdote:

One day I accidentally drove the SWAT van the wrong way on a one-way street. Got confused. To get out of it, I immediately pulled to the side of the road, jumped out, and began peering over a concrete block wall.

So did everyone else who was near enough to see. Then, at the next squawk of the radio, I jumped back in the van and drove off — the correct way. Nobody there knew what happened, but they were glad to have been part of it.

• • •

Detective Davis also passed on this little pearl:

One of our officers, who was not known to be exceptionally bright, stopped a speeding vehicle one cold but very clear night. He walked up to the driver's side of the car and moved his right hand in a circular motion as he mouthed silently the words, "Roll down your window." The driver, a well-to-do woman, just looked at him.

Once again he made the circular motion with his hands, but this time in a very loud voice commanded, "ROLL DOWN YOUR WINDOW!" The driver replied, "It *is* down, you idiot!"

The cop walked away without saying a word, got into his car and drove off.

• • •

Donald Mungham was a policeman in Orillia, Ontario, from 1965 to 1975. He tells us about a case that stands out in his memory:

During the late sixties and early seventies the Orillia police force had a rather primitive radar unit. It consisted of a two-shelf steel table on which was placed a twelve-volt battery (on the lower shelf) and the radar unit was put on the upper shelf. The speed indicator could be locked on by pressing a button at the highest speed recorded, then the police officer would step off the curb and direct the offender to the roadside. The officer would be without radio contact or cruiser, as a corporal would have driven him to the designated location.

On one such occasion I was located on a secondary street where there had been citizen complaints of speeding autos. I had just set up the unit when I observed a green sports car coming up the hill. The speed indicator showed that the vehicle was approaching at forty-eight miles an hour.

I waved it to the curb and observed a very attractive female driver, dressed in summer attire of halter top and cutoff jeans. As an officer who believed in fighting the forces of evil and aiding the downtrodden and oppressed, I retrieved my ticket book and stationed myself at the driver's-side door to keep the offender within easy visual observation.

In some cases, a break was given to speeders and the charge of speeding in a 30 mph zone was reduced. In this instance I decided to lower her speed to 40 mph, thus ensuring her no demerit points.

The young lady was issued a traffic ticket for the speeding offence, and after a lecture on the perils of speed and a brief description of the judicial system, this very attractive offender was allowed to leave.

The next day I was approached by the chief of police, who had checked the day's tickets submitted for court process.

"This speeder was very good-looking, right?" said the chief.

"Do you know her?" I asked.

"No," he replied, "but look at your ticket."

I could see at a glance I'd goofed. I had charged this Venus with driving 30 mph in a 40 mph zone. Case dismissed!

• • •

From 1979 to 1981 Stuart Armstrong, of Oakville, Ontario, was a young constable in Essex, England, stationed near London's east end. He recalls an incident in 1980:

One day when I was on duty driving a cruiser, a very attractive young lady passed me in her car. In my haste to catch up to her I hit the bus in front of me. Thankfully, there wasn't much damage, and I was able to talk my way out of it by saying I was on an emergency call at the time. Of course, by the time the accident was sorted out, the girl of my dreams was long gone. Alas, I never saw her again.

• • •

An attractive young speeder — I'll call her Ingrid — has decided to, uh, expose herself. She's publicly fessing up to her shameful driving practices — with particular reference to the events that took place over a half-hour period one chaotic afternoon . . .

I Kept Meeting All These Nice Cops

My driving record gives a whole new meaning to the term "frequent flyer."

Several years ago, I borrowed my boyfriend's car and assured him I'd return in time to pick him up from work at five p.m. While out touring, I totally forgot about the time, and when I decided to head back it was three-thirty and I had a two-hour drive ahead of me. I thought if I hurried I might be able to get back by five. So I pressed the pedal to the metal and cruised along at 120 kph. It wasn't long before I saw those big red lights behind me. I became quite flustered and pulled over.

As the officer approached, I decided I needed to take advantage of my "cry on the spot" talent. The officer told me I was travelling above the speed limit and asked me what my hurry was. With tears streaming down my contorted face, I wailed a lengthy explanation about how I had to get back to pick up my boyfriend and he'd be really mad if I didn't get back in time and I didn't know I was speeding and I can't afford a ticket and I'm just a student who can hardly afford to eat and just this once I was speeding and I won't ever do it again, so help me God!

The officer listened patiently and then said, "All right, I'll make this a warning, but you be sure to slow down." I thanked him and he returned to his car. I sighed with relief and then had to chuckle. That was pretty easy, I thought.

I followed the speed limit for about ten minutes, then feeling assured that the officer was well out of range, I again began speeding — a little faster than before, to make up for lost time.

Suddenly I saw another set of red lights behind me. I wondered if this was the same officer I'd just met. When the cruiser didn't pass me and his siren became louder, I realized I was being pulled over again. Luckily it was a different policeman. So I began my tearful explanation again, and again the officer listened patiently and miraculously let me go with a warning!

After being stopped twice, I was certain that the chances of getting nailed three times in a very short period on the same highway would be almost nil. As soon as I was out of sight of the officer, I again began to speed.

I couldn't believe my eyes as I came over a hill and saw a cruiser racing towards me. I braked immediately, hoping the cops wouldn't catch me. I slowed down considerably as he sped past. Since he didn't flash his lights, I figured I was safe. How wrong I was! A few seconds later those red lights were right behind me again. I couldn't believe this was happening! I figured my tears had helped me so much before, I'd use the technique again.

This officer was well briefed, it turns out. He came up to my window, looked straight into my teary eyes, and as I sniffled away he smiled and said, "Those tears won't work with me, young lady. I've heard a lot about you in the last little while!"

He wrote me out a ticket and I drove at the speed limit all the rest of the way.

• • •

A fellow we met earlier in this chapter, Kirk J. Roncskevitz, has been a member of the Nashville Police Department in Tennessee for the past six years. Before that, he was a state trooper in Miami, Florida, for five years, and he also served as a policeman in Lewisburg, Tennessee, for about a year. He's talked to a lot of speeders in his day, often in a scholarly or humorous manner, and he's kept notes on many of his memorable roadside confabs. Here are a few he's preserved for posterity:

• Miami, Florida — (105 mph in a 55 mph zone) — A Latin male explained in broken English that he had an "explosion" in his engine. I responded that it was an interesting concept, but an explosion would generally be followed by an immediate loss of power and deceleration.

• Miami, Florida — speeding (95 in a 55) — When this cruise-ship employee came to a stop, he said he was doing the speed limit according to the I-95. I told him that was the interstate sign and said we were both lucky he hadn't exited onto I-395 a mile prior to the stop.

• Lewisburg, Tennessee (50 in a 35) — A woman was stopped for speeding in a residential neighbourhood. She told me she had hit a patch of ice that caused her to speed up. I responded that I could understand how a dramatic reduction in the drag coefficient could cause a temporary acceleration; however, I had paced her up and down hills for three blocks.

• • •

Kathleen Park, of Bristol, England, sends this reminiscence:

My late husband, Clifford, was a police motorcycle officer and wore a peaked cap and goggles. The elastic on the goggles fitted around the band at the back of his cap. Sadly the elastic perished, and there was no way I was going to buy new elastic when the sergeant's wife could give me some — even though it was maroon in colour.

The thirty-miles-an-hour speed limit in "built-up areas" was introduced, and shortly thereafter Clifford was passing through a village when he was overtaken by a motorist, who was duly stopped and summoned to appear at Dursley police court.

When asked in court why he overtook a police patrol in a built-up area, the accused replied, "I didn't know he was a police officer, what with the maroon band he had on his cap. I thought he was in the Salvation Army."

• • •

Toronto accountant Sidney Laufer has no trouble accounting for the warm feeling he was suddenly stricken with one early morning in 1967:

I was blessed with the birth of my son, and I had been working late every night while he and my wife were still in the hospital. Between visiting them and keeping my work up-to-date, I was extremely tired, and this particular night I left the office about

1:00 a.m. I drove up one of Toronto's main streets and, as traffic was almost nonexistent, at a speed greater than the limit.

A police officer pulled me over and began questioning me as to where I was going and whether I knew the speed I'd been driving. I explained what had occurred during the day and said I was very tired and had no idea what my speed was — I just wanted to get home and dive into bed.

The officer looked at me and said he wouldn't give me a ticket.

"But," he warned, "if you don't slow down you may not be around for your son's bar mitzvah."

We both had a good laugh and I drove home — more slowly and carefully than I had before."

• • •

Seventy-six-year-old Mrs. G. C. Williams, of Port Hastings, Nova Scotia, sure knows how to conquer folks with a quip. She wrote to me about one particular instance:

Back when I was only seventy, I was stopped by a couple of Mounties for speeding. One of them said, "What's your hurry, lady?" and I replied, "My dear boys, if you were as old as I am you'd be in a rush, too, because you don't know how much time you've got left."

• • •

Over the years, countless alleged culprits have stood at the bar of justice and advanced the kookiest "reasons" for performing this or that illicit act, from murder all the way down to jaywalking and unauthorized parking. But some excuses, however daffy, have the ring of honesty.

For instance, about thirty years ago a man charged with speeding told St. Boniface, Manitoba, Justice of the Peace Charles M. Bauer, "I was running out of gas and was in a rush to get to the gas station."

• • •

Chief Judge Hazen Strange of the Provincial Court of New Brunswick told me a gripping tale in 1989. It concerned a teenage motorist who was charged with squealing his tires — said dastardly offence having been committed on the night of the annual high-school formal dance. The case was heard in a tiny New Brunswick town.

When all the sordid details of the case had been presented in evidence, the lad threw himself on the mercy of the court, proclaiming with great passion, "I probably did squeal my tires, Your Honour, but I didn't do it on purpose. I'd just pulled up to the gym when I looked down and noticed that I had my old sneakers on — and the prom had already started.

"You see, Your Honour, this was a very formal dance. I had to get home as soon as possible to put on my *new* sneakers."

• • •

In 1993 a priest was one of the winners in a *Toronto Star* contest in which each entrant was asked to send columnist George Gamester "the best excuse you ever gave, got, or heard."

The Reverend Martin Pereira, of Our Lady of the Airways parish in Malton, Ontario, told Gamester and his readers he'd discovered, in effect, that no matter what one's excuse might be, sometimes one just doesn't have a prayer. He explained:

Once, in a busy downtown parish, I had to visit and bring the sacraments to a sick person. But I could find no place to park. Finally I double-parked and left this note on my windshield:

"This is a priest. I circled the area for 20 minutes, but could not find a spot. Will be back in five minutes. Forgive us our trespasses. . ."

When I returned a few minutes later, I found I'd received a parking ticket and a note, which read:

"I have been patrolling this area for 20 years and have not forgiven a single ticket. To do so might cost me my job. Therefore, lead us not into temptation."

• • •

Maggie Preston of Toronto sent me this tender, touching tale:

A few years ago a friend of mine attended a Good Friday morning service, but on her way home she drove through a stop sign.

A police officer zoomed up on his motorcycle and started to write a traffic ticket. My friend pleaded with him.

"Oh, Officer," she wailed, "please don't give me a ticket! It's such a beautiful day. I've been to church, and the music was so wonderful. And, after all, it *is* Good Friday, the day Jesus died on the cross for us."

"Sorry, lady," said the policeman, while handing her the ticket, "but He was just doing His job, and I'm doing mine."

• • •

RCMP constable Duncan Chisholm, who appears often in these pages, always laughs when he's reminded of this next case:

One summer's day in 1990, while on radar patrol in Port Rexton, Newfoundland, I caught a fellow for speeding. I walked up to his car and was about to ask him for his driver's licence, registration, and insurance when out of the blue he said, "I'll have a Big Mac, a large order of fries, and a Coke to go."

I roared with laughter, told him it was the best line I'd heard in a long time, and let him go.

Well, two months later I was doing radar patrol again and, lo and behold, along came the same car and driver, speeding again. I walked up to the vehicle, standing a bit farther back than I had before so he couldn't see me, and automatically he came out with the exact same "order" he'd given on the earlier occasion.

I leaned down with a big smile on my face and when he saw me he simply smiled back and said, "Aw, shucks!"

• • •

In the 1970s, Corporal (now Sergeant) Patrick A. McBride of Matsqui, British Columbia, read that a certain police magazine was sponsoring a contest to find "the most creative excuse for speeding ever heard." Pat entered the contest and won it, hands down, with this true-life adventure story.

And Away We Go!

Dusk was falling on a late summer's evening in a rural area of Matsqui when a patrolling police officer came into contact with a speeder and activated his emergency equipment. The offending vehicle responded to this show of authority by increasing its speed — and the chase was on.

It was about ten o'clock and light was fading fast, making driving conditions on an unlit country road a trifle hazardous. At speeds of between 80 and 90 mph, the driver of the offending vehicle realized he was not outrunning the police vehicle and, instead of speed, resorted to camouflage — by turning off his headlights and so blending more with the darkening countryside.

Deprived of illumination, he began to run a little close to the road edge, with the result that he demolished a school-bus shelter, followed closely by several mailboxes.

He was now hampered in his headlong flight by failing natural light, no artificial light, bus shelter, and mailboxes, so he sought the more pleasant and spacious surroundings of a local field, occupied by several members of the bovine species. Entry was made through a gate which, to this day, has never been replaced.

On entering this more peaceful setting, he quickly dispatched a huge member of the herd to that big pasture in the sky. This was a humane death, with the animal being hit at about 80 mph and being deposited on the roof of the vehicle. As a result of the collision, the hood opened, revealing that the engine was on fire.

On being further hampered by the still-failing light, no head-lights, bus shelter, mailboxes, gate, cows, smoke from the engine, and now the hood being up against the windshield, the driver was maintaining a good rate of speed through the rest of the scattering herd.

Finally, after ploughing through one last fence and entering a berry field, the vehicle raced towards its final objective, a house. Alas, the engine had given its utmost and, slowed down by soft ground, berry wire, posts, and berries, it finally gave up three yards short of the living-room wall.

The car was burning merrily by this time, adding a certain glow to the proceedings.

As the constable dashed forward, he saw a figure crouching on the floor of the vehicle, with the doors locked from within. A terrible threat was made, providing the occupant with the nec-essary initiative to release himself from his fiery pyre.

Upon opening the door the speeder uttered these immortal words: "Please, sir, no bullshit, if I'd known you wished me to stop, I would've stopped a lot sooner."

3

PRANKS AND OTHER SHENANIGANS

For Satan finds some mischief still
For idle hands to do.
— Isaac Watts (1674-1748)

Not every police officer is a practising prankster. But it often seems that way.

Experts who've studied the phenomenon of people horsing around while on duty have concluded that it's caused by two old foes of the working man or woman — stress and boredom.

Police work has plenty of both, to be sure. When a cop isn't racing to the scene of a crime, uncertain of what awaits, he or she is often driving around, especially late at night, bored to tears. Both situations demand some form of temporary relief. So that's *why* coppers the world over indulge rather regularly in monkeyshines and tomfoolery. Now let's see *how* they do it.

Retired Toronto police sergeant Jack Burton, of Lindsay, Ontario, wrote to me to describe a cheeky courtroom caper that occurred in Toronto in the early 1960s:

The scene is Courtroom 22 at the Old City Hall at Bay and Queen streets, which, being a court for "first time up" cases, was usually packed with lawyers and accused persons seeking adjournments. On the day in question, all the seats at the counsel table and in the gallery were occupied, and it was standing room only in the spacious courtroom.

A very young lawyer entered the court, scanned the crowd, and suddenly spotted a seat on the far side of the room. The vacancy was at the end of a long bench-type oaken seat. At one end sat three rather large police officers in uniform. This seat was situated at the front of the courtroom, just to the side of the Crown attorney.

The only reason the end seat was unoccupied was that every police officer knew there was a crack in the bench, and when weight was applied at the other end the crack would open up, and when the weight was lifted the crack would snap shut. The Crown attorneys also knew about the crack.

As the rookie lawyer walked across the front of the courtroom, the prosecutor and the three policemen, as well as numerous other informed parties, eyed him with what appeared to be keen anticipation. As the lawyer sat down with a look of satisfaction on his face, senior magistrate Thomas S. Elmore was proceeding furiously with the job of setting trial dates. About five minutes later, the three burly police officers leaned ahead at the same time, taking the weight off the bench.

The crack grabbed the young lawyer by a cheek. He gave a yelp of pain, and then the three officers sat back.

The courtroom broke into laughter, including the magistrate, who had to take a recess to compose himself.

During the lunch break that day, on the instructions of Magistrate Elmore, workmen stashed the old oak bench in the city hall's cavernous attic, where it still sits, gathering dust.

• • •

In his autobiography, *Copper Jack*, former inspector Jack Webster, chief of the Toronto Homicide Squad in the late 1960s and early 1970s, writes about his colleague, Staff Superintendent and Chief of Detectives Adolphus Payne, whom he described as "the finest detective Canada has ever produced." Webster hastens to add that Payne was a peerless prankster:

I recall a practical joke this famous man played on unsuspecting colleagues at the scene of a murder. The victim had lived alone, and the body had been lying undiscovered for over a week. Decomposition had set in and neither the sight nor the smell of the scene was very appealing. On the unlit stove in the kitchen there was a rusty frying pan, with the mouldy, foul-smelling remains of some type of food.

We were joined at the scene by Staff Superintendent Payne. After looking around, he decided that we needed help to make a proper search of the less than tidy premises. Staff Payne left orders with the uniformed officers on guard at the front door to send the two new detectives into the kitchen to see him.

In the meantime, Payne took a dirty plate, piled some of this awful-looking, mouldy, insect-infested food onto it, put the frying pan on the table beside him, got a knife and fork, and sat down. As the two detective reinforcements came into the kitchen, Staff Payne put his tongue in his cheek to extend it, to give the appearance that he had a mouthful of food. He then waved the fork at the detectives and said in a garbled voice, "I'm just having my supper, won't you sit down and join me?"

The officers looked at the food, got a whiff of the awful smell, and promptly threw up. They had to be assisted outside to the fresh air, and absolutely refused to re-enter the premises. The staff superintendent and the rest of us laughed for ten minutes straight, and Payne said, "They don't make detectives like they used to."

Some people reading this may feel that this was a poor demonstration of humour for a senior officer to make during a serious investigation. To these people I can only say that if you have never been present at an investigation of this type, you wouldn't understand how much you need a good laugh from time to time.

• • •

Staff Sergeant Steve Hibbard of the Waterloo Regional Police Service in Cambridge, Ontario, files this report about an historic battle in an ancient war that will probably go on forever:

Police constables have always accepted the challenge of out-witting their sergeants, whose sole mission in life, it appears, is to catch a constable napping on the midnight shift or meeting with another constable for a clandestine coffee klatch.

A number of years ago, a Waterloo sergeant saw two cruisers enter a cemetery in the wee morning hours. The cruisers drove to the back of the cemetery, shutting off their lights as they pulled in behind the crematorium.

The sergeant, hoping to catch the constables with coffee and doughnuts in hand — the sly game of Gotcha! never seems to end — started a slow approach with his lights off. He was unaware that one of the constables had seen him earlier and arranged this meeting to turn the tables.

As the sergeant drove into the cemetery, the constables slipped out unseen and padlocked the gates behind them.

The sergeant was placed in the embarrassing situation of calling the dispatcher over the police radio to get someone from

the city staff out of bed to unlock the gates. No one ever identified those constables, but their feat is legendary.

• • •

In the previous chapter you met Stuart Armstrong of Oakville,
Ontario, who was a constable in Essex, England, from 1979 to
1981. He has many fond memories of his stint there — especially the tomfoolery that frequently erupted late at night.

"One night my partner and I got balloons and squeeze bottles, which we filled up with water," Stuart says. "We drove up to
some fellow officers, lured them out of the car, and bombarded
them with water. This began a two-week period of water fights
and sneak attacks, culminating in a 'terrorist' attack on the
police station at 3:00 a.m.

"It was nice to know that while crime was running rampant in
the streets, constables were performing their duties responsibly."

• • •

Chris Perkins is a detective constable with the fraud unit of the
Halton Regional Police in Oakville, Ontario. But from 1980 to
1989 he served with the Metropolitan Police (aka Scotland Yard
and the Met) in London, England, where, he says, pranks often
became pitched battles in a war that's been raging, with occasional brief truces, for decades:

Night duty became very boring sometimes, and we often dreamt
up pranks and contests to while away the hours. This started
as the not-so-unusual water fights. We'd each fill up several bottles with water and drive around soaking each other at every
opportunity. The foot-beat officers were the most vulnerable,
particularly the young ones, because the police cars could creep
up on them and pretend they were offering a cosy car ride for a
few minutes. Every young officer felt honoured that an old sweat
(a copper who had more than eighteen months' service) would

talk to him, let alone offer a ride in a car. Of course, as soon as the poor sod got within range, the bottles came out and he was soaked before he had time to realize what was happening.

This became a monthly "week of nights" ritual — until some bright spark got the idea that we could club together as a station army and declare war on the neighbouring police station. The telex operator carefully worded a declaration of war, complete with some insulting comments, and sent it off to the next station in our district. And the battle was on!

We were able to communicate on our personal radio channel, but they couldn't hear us, and vice versa, so it was very much a war of strategy and tactics. After a few nights of this spectacular enterprise, we received a telex from the enemy, stating that they had kidnapped one of our young rookies. Sure enough, a search of his beat turned up nothing, and before long we were being taunted as a "bunch of wankers" over his personal radio.

Hearing those comments convinced us that they really did have one of ours. Some old wag sent a message back that they could keep him. However, station pride took over and we decided a rescue was called for. They issued demands over the telex machine and we agreed to some of them — provided they released our man. A mutual location was agreed upon, and we were told in no uncertain terms that if we attempted an ambush they would keep him for the rest of the night in one of their cells.

Of course we weren't going to be bullied into accepting those terms, and we set up troops in hidden places suitable for an ambush at the designated release location, which was on the border between the two areas. At the appointed time their station van turned up and stopped in the middle of the street. Uncertain whether the van doors would fling open to reveal overwhelming numbers of the enemy, we held off the attack.

The van doors did eventually open, and a long metal pole was poked out the rear. Then the doors opened a little more, and the young PC was unceremoniously pushed out the back, handcuffed to the pole, naked apart from his underwear. The van sped off and the pole was pulled through the handcuffs, leaving the poor young bastard standing there freezing cold in the middle of the street.

We bombarded the van as it drove by, but I think they won that campaign. The water fights ended soon after, when we discovered that Met Police property bags made great weapons when filled with water and flung off high buildings. The next day there was a complaint from a citizen who'd found loads of MP plastic bags strewn all over the place, and, alas, that put a close to those fights.

• • •

Keith Edwards. Now *there's* a bloke who knows how to liven things up on a boring night at the cop shop. Keith's a sergeant with the Met in London, operating out of the Peckham station, but the elaborate prank he's so justly proud of took place a few years ago when he was stationed at Bexleyheath in southeast London.

I was working the night shift and things were quiet and uneventful. I volunteered to relieve our communications officer, Alison, while she took her refreshment break. In her absence I decided to concoct a message, purely for her amusement, and I left it on the message pad and awaited her return. The note simply read that a Mrs. Smart had reported three elephants roaming free around Dartford Heath, an open space used mainly as a sports ground, and requested that police attend to deal with these stray beasts. I used the name Smart because it's also the name of a famous British circus company called Billy Smarts.

When Alison returned she read the message and knew immediately it was a hoax. But then entered Police Constable Mark Milton, the unwitting star of the show. Mark asked if he could help with anything. He was told about the elephant message and, to everyone's surprise, he said, "Okay, I'll take a look at that," and left the station. The conspirators couldn't pass up such an opportunity, so they got to work.

They phoned Dartford Police in the nearby Kent constabulary to advise that one of their men would soon join Dartford colleagues in a search for a small herd of elephants — and they asked that an audience be sent pronto. Meanwhile, PC Milton was temporarily delayed at Sidcup Police Station prior to his visit to Dartford Heath.

To keep things moving, I rang a colleague at Plumstead Police Station, whose voice would be unknown to PC Milton, and asked her to call Sidcup police to complain of a slow police response to her original call. She did a fine job, stating that she was Mrs. Smart and she was now concerned for her son, Billy, who had himself gone to seek the elephants and had failed to return. On learning this, PC Milton informed us by radio that he was now making his way to the heath.

All the night shift now knew what was going on, including PC Paul Williams, who called Mark to say he'd pick him up in his car and speed him to the scene. WPC Jo Sillitoe was at the time on the phone to a colleague in north London and informed her of events. She in turn gathered other officers around the phone so they could listen in on our radio transmissions via the radio handset Jo was holding against her phone.

Two of our patrol cars, containing five officers, including myself, then made their way up to the darkest parts of the heath and concealed themselves there. Once we'd parked, we noticed two officers with torches running around the heath, and later learned that the officer we'd informed in Dartford had thought it a fine ruse. Instead of sending his colleagues to go and watch the fun, he'd dispatched a car to search for the elephants. They soon appeared to give up and drove away. Then PC Williams arrived in his car and radioed to say he was dropping Mark off so he could start his search. Meanwhile, PC Williams pretended to make his way to search from the far side.

We eagerly awaited the appearance of Mark as he neared us in our hiding place, and as soon as we saw his torchlight, the five of us, now in one car, had to work hard to suppress our laughter. Then Sergeant Brian Cherek reached for the vehicle's PA system and emitted several realistic-sounding elephant-trumpeting noises. We saw PC Milton stop and then, incredibly, heard him radio our Control Room and report, "They're definitely here — I can hear sounds reminiscent of elephants."

Brian continued to trumpet over the PA system until Mark got so close to us we feared he'd see the vehicles. So the five of us gathered around the car's radio handset and broadcast over the heath a little ditty we'd composed for the occasion — "Oooooohhhhhh, Nellie the Elephant packed her trunk and said goodbye to the circus" — and then collapsed in hysterics.

A few weeks later we held our team's Christmas party at a local restaurant. I'd organized it and urged everyone to attend in formal attire. I made sure I was the last to arrive as I had hired a pink elephant costume. I walked into the restaurant and loudly demanded, "Is there a Mark Milton here?"

You should have seen his face. But he was a good sport and saw the funny side of it, as he'd done with his Search for the Elephants.

• • •

Jerry Bledsoe, chief of police in Chaffee, Missouri, is well aware of the therapeutic value of a chuckle — even if it doesn't tickle a fine, feathered friend. He wrote to me with the following tail — I mean, tale:

During the mid-1980s a close friend of mine and I were employed by the Scott County, Missouri, Sheriff's Department as road deputies. Most of the employees at the department would from time to time pull pranks on each other to break the monotony.

65

Late one afternoon, just after dark, we were at the county jail when I noticed two large sets of fluffy, colourful feathers held together with leather strings and clips. The feathers had been seized at a carnival because of drug residue on the clips, but no charges were filed, and the feathers were left hanging in the firearms locker at the jail. As soon as I saw them, I had a brainstorm.

When my friend (in full uniform) turned his back and spoke to another officer, I clipped both sets of feathers on his duty belt in the rear, and he had no idea I'd done this. A few minutes later we were dispatched to a rural address where there'd been a bicycle theft. By then I'd completely forgotten about the feathers, but as we entered the house we'd been sent to, I couldn't help noticing them. It was too late. There was nothing I could do but leave the feathers in place.

Inside, we met a man, his wife, and two curious young children. While my friend was asking questions, he was moving around a lot and doing a great job of displaying the feathers. One of the children followed my friend around the living room staring at the feathers, and I was about to bust a gut laughing. Unknowingly, my friend got the attention of the entire family with his colourful display. As we were exiting the house with the man, I could hear the children and their mother snickering in the background.

Outside, I removed the feathers from my friend's belt. He felt this action and turned to me with a startled look. The man and I both busted out laughing while my friend appeared to be in a daze. He said we were supposed to be professionals, and walking around with feathers hanging from one's belt didn't look very professional.

I said, "Listen, friend, take a bow. These folks were victims of a crime that left them feeling very sad, and you came along, God bless you, and lifted their spirits and made them happy again for a while."

Somehow I don't think he bought that.

• • •

Cops and criminal lawyers sometimes pull pranks on each other right in the middle of a trial. In a 1982 trial, for instance, Ottawa lawyer Lawrence Greenspon provoked gales of laughter with an extremely short cross-examination.

A policeman testified that he had fingerprinted and photographed Greenspon's client. Since he admitted the man's qualifications as an identification officer, the lawyer didn't really have any questions to ask him. But he decided to have some fun.

A few weeks earlier, Greenspon had attended an evening of entertainment presented by the Ottawa Police Male Choir. The identification officer had worn a wedding dress in one of the skits.

"Officer, I understand you're a member of the Ottawa Police Force," counsel began.

"Yes, sir, I am."

"And either in that capacity, or in any other capacity, have you ever had occasion to wear a dress?"

"Pardon?"

"Have you ever had occasion to wear a dress?"

"Yes, sir, I have."

"Okay. I have no other questions."

• • •

Criminal lawyers often rile police witnesses by cross-examining them ferociously about the notes they made at the time of, or right after, their investigation.

Judge Stewart Fisher, of Milton, Ontario, tells about the time the noted Toronto criminal lawyer David G. Humphrey (now Mr. Justice Humphrey) was grilling a veteran detective, as he had many times in the past, about what notes he'd made pertaining to various important matters.

"The police officer kept referring to his notebook," recalls Judge Fisher, "and David asked him if he could examine the contents of the book."

The cop consented and, smiling slyly, handed the book to Humphrey.

"It was blank," says His Honour, "except for the words,"F——you, Humphrey, got you this time!' "

Naturally Humphrey didn't wish to give the cop any satisfaction, so he turned the pages slowly, appearing to read various entries, then handed the book back to his tormentor and said casually, as he strolled away from the witness box, "Thank you very much, Officer."

• • •

Several years ago, at a San Diego police precinct called Western, a gripping drama unfolded. The editor of the police department's newsletter, *Up Front*, describes it thus:

Mike Carleton (legal adviser) made the unhappy mistake of leaving his "duck cup" at Western. The detectives found it in the kitchen. (Guess that's why they're detectives.) They decided that the only reasonable course of action was to hold it for ransom and sent several sets of instructions to Mike on how to retrieve it.

When that was unsuccessful, they bought six similar cups and did a photo lineup. Alas, Mike couldn't make a positive identification. The next step was a morning meeting when *all* the Western detectives had duck cups. Finally, two months later, the original duck cup was returned for a ransom of two dozen doughnuts.

• • •

Former Windsor, Ontario, policeman Al Porter, whom we met earlier, regales us with this cheeky anecdote:

In 1976 the Ontario Provincial Police trained a number of officers from a municipal force to ride motorcycles on their annual course at the Ontario Police College in Aylmer. On the second-last day of one of the courses, one of the instructors left his camera on the front seat of his cruiser while he walked back to his office to complete some paperwork. The trainees were supposed to be rehearsing their graduation routine.

As soon as the instructor was out of sight, two of the municipal officers grabbed his camera and an OPP golden helmet and disappeared into one of the old aircraft hangars. One of the municipal officers just happens to have a large blue eyeball tattooed on each cheek of his buttocks. He immediately dropped his coveralls, then the other officer placed the OPP helmet on the small of his colleague's back and took some quick photos. The pair returned the camera to its place in the cruiser.

A few weeks later the officer with the tattoos received a telephone call from the instructor advising that he had turned in the film to the identification section at OPP general headquarters, and it had been developed and printed there. He was summoned to the commissioner's office to pick up his prints, as the ident officer had called his supervisor and the photos had quickly made their way up the OPP chain of command to the commissioner's office. Everyone along the way wanted to know, "Who's the asshole in the OPP helmet?"

• • •

Al Porter returns with:

The Great Coca Cola Caper

A certain officer on the Windsor police force, affectionately known as Staff Sergeant Von Psycho, became famous as one who'd actually fulfilled the fantasy of everyone who's ever been ripped off by a vending machine. One day, the Coca-Cola machine in the police lunch room did something it had done many times before — it stole Von Psycho's quarter. Whereupon he drew his gun (no reports required in those days) and pumped six rounds into the #&!@zx%*$! machine.

As Von Psycho's retirement grew nigh, a couple of cops persuaded the general manager of the Coca-Cola bottling plant to
donate the front of an old Coke machine. A few nights later his
entire shift went to the shooting range and emptied their
revolvers into the door, which shortly thereafter was presented
to the boss at his retirement party.

• • •

An Edmonton, Alberta, cop tells a tale about two of his colleagues who chanced upon a slumbering drunk in a scrapyard.

The man was lying on his back, resplendent in a clean white T-
shirt. The officers fetched an old truck tire, then rolled it through
a mud puddle and across the man's chest. Then they woke him
up and asked him if he was okay. Upon seeing the tire mark on
his shirt, the drunk began to boast about how rugged he was.

The trick kind of backfired, however, when the fellow shuffled
off to the nearby police headquarters to report a hit and run.
Now there was a lot more work to do.

• • •

Officer Kirk Roncskevitz, of Nashville, Tennessee, has another
story for us, this one about a friend of his, a Florida cop named
Jim Carr, who's an incurable prankster:

Jim had the funniest gag I can remember. He had a Styrofoam
head used to display wigs. He put some Halloween hair on it,
painted it and made a face on it, and from time to time he'd place
it in strategic places where it would cause the greatest alarm.

I once had the privilege of watching Jim in action. A towtruck
driver responded to a call to tow a car that was parked on the
side of the highway. When the driver bent down to secure the
chain-hook under the car, he discovered the "head" wedged
under a tire. He let out a bloodcurdling scream and jumped off
the ground.

The memory of this frolic still brings a chuckle today, ten years later.

• • •

Detective Terry L. Davis, of Lemoore, California, is also addicted to pranks — especially the kind that conveys a subtle message. Like the two he describes here:

A married sergeant who decided he would visit his girlfriend while on duty got caught, big time. Officers saw his patrol unit parked on the street in front of her apartment building. They decided to make this sergeant aware that everybody knew.

After lighting fifteen or so road flares and placing them all around his car, we had the dispatcher leave him an important message, which he got when he returned to his vehicle. He was quiet the whole shift and had a corporal handle that night's debriefing!

• • •

Terry Davis tells us about another educational caper:

We found a security guard asleep in one of the cars on the lot he was supposed to be guarding. We took a few Polaroids of him and stuck them under the windshield wiper so they'd be the first thing he saw upon awakening. I wonder how many shifts he started with the fear that another copy would be on his boss's desk when he walked in.

• • •

Pro that he is, Detective Davis also appreciates the artistic work of imaginative fellow pranksters:

One of our officers found a sickly chicken that had wandered away from the local chicken-processing plant. The dispatcher on duty was unbelievably naive, and the officer was about to take advantage of that.

He grabbed the chicken and put it in the back of his patrol car. He then drove to the police station and placed the bird on the booking counter.

"Book it!" he ordered.

The dispatcher said, "What? What for?"

The officer said, "Never mind, I'll do it myself!" And, with that, he put the chicken in a holding cell. He then left.

He drove to the fire department and got one of the firemen, who was a good straightman, to make a phone call to dispatch. The fireman called the dispatcher and demanded to know why his chicken had been arrested, what the bail was, and whether he could have visitors, and, if so, when.

Proof of the dispatcher's gullibility came when he did his best to try to calm the caller and promised he'd find out why the chicken had been arrested.

• • •

And here's one more tale from Terry Davis:

Slapstick in the Sticks

As part of his patrol of rural areas of the county, a deputy-sheriff friend of mine made a point of always checking a particular shed on a farmer's land. There was an expensive herbicide stored in the shed and it had been burglarized before — primarily because it was so far from the farmhouse.

One night, when checking the shed, the deputy's headlights caught the reflectors on the side of a vehicle. He approached on foot. A California state patrol vehicle was parked between two fifteen-foot-high stacks of hay. An officer was asleep in the back seat, with his feet hanging out the door. Another was in a similar position on the front seat. The gun belts of both men were lying across the hood of the car.

The deputy realized he had a rare opportunity not only to teach

these idiots a lesson, but also to get back at the state patrol officers who always seemed to find work for the deputy sheriffs. He
pulled out his semiautomatic "varmint rifle" that he always carried
in his trunk (when graveyard shifts got slow, he shot at rabbits in
the fields) and discharged six rounds in rapid succession. What
happened next would have made the greatest film in history.

The snoozing cops both jumped up and out and promptly ran
into each other — both falling as a result. They then began looking
for their gun belts — in fact, one officer ran around the car three
times before he recalled that the things were on the engine hood.

The deputy soon began laughing, and the troopers knew
they'd been had, big time. But their sense of humour had vanished. They screamed abuse at the deputy, who smiled and said
sweetly, "The Polaroids are safe with me." He then drove off.

These guys were all good friends after that. Finally a strong
working relationship developed between the state patrol and the
sheriff's department.

• • •

Meet Hugh Valance Brown, a former member of the Metropolitan
Police (Scotland Yard or the Met) in London, England. Hughie,
as everyone calls him, joined that world-famous organization as
a cadet in 1959 and retired as a sergeant in 1973. He has a
wealth of funny stories from those years and I've scattered them
throughout this book, but before we sample a few of them, let's
take a peek at this fun-loving copper's serious side.

"Every police officer starts at the bottom of the ladder and
has an opportunity to work his or her way up and gain invaluable experience while doing so," says Hughie from his home in
Regina, Saskatchewan, where he's been a private investigator
since 1976. "The Metropolitan Police gave me an experience in
life that most people only dream about, and my memories are
but a tiny fraction of what can be told."

For instance, there was a historic event in 1963. "I was sitting in a cruiser with another officer at Euston Station, London," Hughie says, "awaiting the arrival of the train with cash from the northern banks for disposal at the Bank of England. A message came over the radio transmitter for us to cancel our assignment. The train had been stopped and robbed. The Great Train Robbery had happened."

He recalls the bombing of the revolving restaurant at the top of the GPO tower in London; an airlift by the RAF to a coastal town so police could assist the locals in keeping peace between the mods and rockers; the attack on the U.S. Embassy where he got injured; a gunman pointing his loaded weapon at him, and his dive for cover.

But Hughie would much rather recall humorous events, the first of which he narrates now.

It's All in the Interpretation

When a person who doesn't speak English is arrested, it's Scotland Yard policy to call out an interpreter so that charges can be fully understood. Lists of interpreters are kept at every police station.

One Saturday night a drunk was brought into Paddington police station. When questioned by the station officer, it was soon obvious that the drunk could only speak German. The station officer asked around the station if anyone spoke German, but no one was found.

"Call out an interpreter," said the sergeant to his communications officer. A while later the reply came back that no official interpreter was available at the moment.

The station officer had the information room (IR) send a message to all cars, asking if there was a police officer on duty who spoke German and could attend at Paddington station. IR went into action. "All cars, all cars, any unit with an officer on board who can speak German, acknowledge, please."

One car responded immediately in the affirmative. It rushed to Paddington station, and the two officers entered the charge room. They approached a busy sergeant and one of them said, "Skipper, you wanted someone who could speak German?"

"Oh, yes," said the sergeant. "That man over there, he only speaks German. See what you can get out of him."

"Okay," was the response, and they approached the prisoner. One of them grabbed the man by his tie, stood him up, and said in a loud, guttural voice, "UND VAT IS YOUR NAME?"

The prisoner looked stunned. The sergeant's mouth dropped open in astonishment.

"He doesn't even know his own language, Sarge," said one of the wise guys.

"Get out of here, you jerks!" said the sergeant, who then told the communications officer, "Get me a *real* interpreter!"

• • •

Sometimes shenanigans lead to unexpected consequences, as Hughie Brown reveals in this reminiscence.

Just Walkin' in the Rain

Tottenham Court Road police station was a substation to us at Albany Street, and all messages had to be relayed over the phone to them. Leo was attached to Tottenham Court Road station. He was a very nice fellow, but if you said the moon was made out of cheese and kept a straight face, he would probably believe you. I'd have the odd joke with Leo, and he always took it well.

One of the police boundaries was the Euston Road and Tottenham Court Road, and at this juncture there was an underpass for east-west traffic. This particular night I was posted as communications officer at Albany Street, and Leo was posted the same at Tottenham Court Road. It was one of those quiet nights, raining cats and dogs, no one about except patrolling cops, and I'd bet that not many of them were getting wet.

A little boredom set in, so I thought I'd get Leo's adrenalin going a bit. I gave him a call and said, "Leo, we need your help.

A car travelling south has had an accident. It mounted the safety barrier and fell down into the underpass and is lying on its roof." After a short pause, I said, "You got all that written down, Leo?"

"Yes, I have," he replied.

"Well, don't worry," I said, "I'm just joking with you. I wanted you to know what it's like at a busy station."

Leo said, "Sorry, Hughie. While I was writing all that stuff down, Inspector Egan was watching over my shoulder. Once he got the gist of it, he raced out the door and took every available man in the station. They're walking to the scene in the rain."

What the hell have I done? I asked myself. I'm in for it now!

About thirty minutes later, a soaking Inspector Egan walked into the communications room at Albany Street and sputtered, "I've just walked in the rain with half the bloody station to the scene of an accident that did not exist! You'd better have a damn good explanation, Brown!"

"Well, sir," I replied, "the intent was to liven Leo up a little. He sometimes needs a little push, and I thought a small joke might help to pass the time a bit. I had no idea that you were there while he was copying the message down, and I'm sorry you got wet. When I told Leo it was a joke, he told me that you and the others had already left, and I knew I'd be in for it then."

The inspector informed me I was being officially warned about my actions and then quietly added, "Thank God someone has a sense of humour around here!" When I heard that, I knew I was off the hook, and, needless to say, I didn't do that sort of thing again.

• • •

In this adventure story the policeman (Hughie Brown) is the victim, not the instigator, of a memorable piece of tomfoolery.

Don't Be Cheeky

One excruciatingly boring morning, while standing on guard in front of a diplomat's ritzy dwelling, I got drawn into a scrap between a yappy little Scottish terrier that had got loose and an unidentified large sandy-coloured dog on a leash. I had just saved the terrier from a surefire mauling by the far heavier animal when, all of a sudden, the terrier decided to attack *me*!

The dog whipped around and sunk its teeth through my leather glove and into my hand. The sharp teeth felt like red-hot nails. I peeled off my glove and found that my hand was covered with blood and contained about a dozen puncture wounds.

Sergeant Bob Gibson drove me to University College Hospital so I could get a tetanus shot. On the way we passed the Lord Wellington, the pub that most of the doctors, nurses, and other staff used as their watering hole. A few of us cops and our wives frequented it, too, and we were all on first-name terms. One of the patrons of the pub was a nurse named Pat, an extremely pleasant person I figured I might be seeing a few minutes later at the hospital.

I was right. When we entered the emergency section of the hospital, Pat was one of the first people we saw.

"Hello, Hughie. Hello Sarge. What's up?" she asked.

"Dog bite," said Bob. "Need a tetanus shot for him."

"Okay," said Pat. "Get into that cubicle, Hughie, and I'll get authorization from the doctor."

Bob saw me into the cubicle and said, "I'll be outside."

"They give it in the arm now, don't they, Sarge?" I inquired a tad nervously.

"I think they do," he replied.

Just then Pat walked in with a needle in her hand. She grinned and said, "Drop them!"

"In the arm, isn't it, Pat?" I asked anxiously.

Still grinning, she commanded, "Drop them!"

"Come on, Pat," I begged, "this will be all around the pub! They won't give up!"

"Drop them!"

"Please, Pat, you don't really mean that, do you?"

"While you're in here, I'm in charge. Drop them!"

"Okay," I moaned, and I lowered my pants just enough for her to get the needle in. All done. I don't suppose I would have minded if it had been a complete stranger, but this was like dropping your drawers to a neighbour.

Pat was still grinning as she remarked, "It's not every day we get to order a uniformed policeman to drop his trousers." She then cleaned and bandaged my hand and I was free to go.

Right then and there, Sergeant Gibson and I agreed on a drastic course of action. As we started to walk out of the hospital in front of a mob of waiting patients, I put my good hand on the sergeant's shoulder and he put his arm around my waist as if to help me walk. I suddenly developed a terrible limp and, with a look of agony contorting my face, I placed my freshly bandaged hand over my heart.

Sergeant Gibson then asked me in a booming voice, "WHAT THE HELL HAVE THEY DONE TO YOU?" and immediately I replied, in an equally strong voice, "I DON'T KNOW, SARGE, I JUST CAME IN WITH A TOOTHACHE!"

Dead silence. All eyes, including medical staff, were riveted on us as we left the building. I looked back at Pat. Her face was bright red. I turned to the sergeant and said, "I don't think the story of my bare ass will be passed around the pub with much enthusiasm now."

• • •

If Hughie Brown lives to be 150, he'll never forget the uproarious time he and a slew of Met colleagues had late one night at the station. He preserved it all in print, as follows:

Hair We Go

Property found in London taxis must be handed in at any police station. The driver of the cab is then entitled to a reward based on the declared value of the property by the claimant. One extremely peaceful night there were eight uniformed policemen in the front office of the Albany Street station — practically a mob when you consider that it was only 3:00 a.m. Right around that time, while we were all still there, a cab driver came in and placed a large cardboard box on the counter.

"How can a bloke forget anything this big?" he wondered aloud. I said the man probably had other things on his mind, and I then started the paperwork on the property found.

"One sealed box," I murmured, and the driver said, "Yeah, I'll have to open it, mate — you know the rules."

I opened the box in front of the cabbie and found fifteen to twenty assorted colourful theatrical wigs. The contents were listed and the finder signed the papers and left the station.

"What you got, Brown?" the sergeant asked.

"Wigs," I replied.

The sergeant then took out a large Afro-type wig, put it on, and started parading around the office. Howls of laughter broke out, and before long we were all wearing wigs of different shapes and sizes. More howls ensued. I had tears running down my face. Some of the wigs were then exchanged among officers, which made us look like absolute idiots in uniform. I was laughing so hard my stomach hurt.

Another exchange, more laughter. A mini-fashion parade of London's finest, all engrossed in the wacky show they were putting on. If the commissioner of police had been there for those few minutes, he would never have believed that eight of his uniformed officers were wearing wigs and prancing about in a state of near-hysteria.

Suddenly the sergeant whipped off his wig and walked to the counter.

"Yes, sir?" he said.

We all looked around. A smartly dressed gentleman stood before us wearing the most absolute fixed stare of pure amazement I've ever seen. We all removed our wigs, replaced them in the box, and got out of the office, pronto, thus leaving it to the red-faced sergeant to try to give travel directions to the dazed chap at the counter. He pulled it off fairly well, but when his eyes met the visitor's eyes the sarge broke down and cackled uncontrollably.

Serves him right. After all, wearing the wigs was *his* idea.

• • •

When Dwayne Wade Rowe and his law-school classmate Christopher D. Evans practised criminal law together in Calgary, Alberta, from 1979 to 1984, there were many moments of merriment in the office that sprang up suddenly and left everyone energized and happy to get back to work. Like the time a rookie policeman came to the law firm of Evans and Rowe to present Dwayne with a parking ticket.

Dwayne was in the reception room when the officer arrived.

"Excuse me," the policeman said to one of the secretaries. "I'm looking for a Mr. Dwayne Rowe." He was holding a small piece of paper in his hand.

Dwayne turned on his heel, sprinted into his office, locked the door and yelled, "I'm not going back to the Big House! You'll never take me alive, copper!"

The police officer, a fellow who'd seen perhaps nineteen summers, nervously approached the door to communicate with the fugitive from justice.

"Mr. Rowe," he said through the door, "it's only a $5 ticket."

"Get lost, flatfoot!" hollered the man within. "I'm never going back! Do you *hear* me? *Never!*"

The officer slid the ticket under the door and left forthwith.

Judge Rowe, as he is now, still chuckles when he recalls that moment of manufactured pandemonium. "Chris and I did a lot of work for the Calgary Police Association, defending members when they got into trouble," Rowe told me. "The young cop went back and reported to the brass of the association that they were dealing with a lunatic. Of course, he was correct."

• • •

Sergeant Gary Dale, of the Southampton-Port Elgin, Ontario, police service, has many fond memories of escapades he was involved in when he was a constable in the town of Hanover, Ontario, back in the 1970s and early 1980s. Here's his recollection of a prolonged prank calculated to drive his boss bonkers.

Rubik's Bloody Cube

One day in 1980 I was working the day shift with Sergeant Don Deratnay and the chief of police, who shall, mercifully, remain nameless. The sergeant's office was separated from the constables' room by a wall with a sliding glass window.

Things were a bit slow at the office, and I was cleaning out my desk. I came across that maddening little item known to millions as Rubik's Cube. There were different coloured squares on each side of the cube, and the idea of the puzzle was to get all the red squares on one side, the orange squares on another, blue squares on another, and so on. Some people are quite good at doing it, but most of us give up in disgust. I also had a second cube that was lined up with the colours in the correct positions.

I showed Sergeant Deratnay the two cubes, one completed and the other all scrambled up. I told him I was going to get the chief going with these puzzles, but he didn't seem to think my plan would work. I stepped across the hall to the chief's office with the unfinished puzzle in my hand, then asked him, "Have you ever tried to complete one of these Rubik's Cubes?"

The chief looked up from what he was working on and said he hadn't. I advised him that most people have great difficulty completing them. I was twisting the sides of the cube around as I talked and showed the chief what the idea of the puzzle was. As I continued to twist the sides of the puzzle, I stepped back out of his office and across to mine, switching the unfinished cube

81

for the finished cube. About twenty seconds later I stepped back into the chief's office and showed him the finished puzzle, stating that I couldn't see what was so difficult about the darn thing.

I then asked the chief if he'd like to try putting the puzzle together, and he said he'd give it a go. I left the office, pretending to mix up the sides again, and replaced the finished puzzle with the unfinished puzzle. I handed the chief the unfinished puzzle, saying, "Here, give it a try. It's pretty much kid stuff."

The chief started twisting the sides, trying to line up the colours. I put the finished puzzle back in my desk and advised Sergeant Deratnay that I was going out to walk the beat. He smiled and said, "I can't believe you've sucked him in so easily."

I bet Deratnay that the chief would still be working on the puzzle when I returned. Sure enough, when I came back, about two hours later, Deratnay said the chief had just put the puzzle down in frustration. Well, I couldn't leave things just hanging there, so I decided to rub a little salt into the wound.

I went into the chief's office and picked up the unfinished puzzle from his desk. I asked him politely if he'd had any trouble with the puzzle, and he said, "Yeah, I couldn't get the stupid thing." I walked out of his office, rotating the sides of the puzzle as if trying to solve it while returning to my desk.

Once again I switched the unfinished puzzle, with the finished puzzle and a couple of minutes later I returned to the chief's office to show him how simple the puzzle was.

I left his office, did another quick switcheroo, and returned again while rotating the sides. Sergeant Deratnay and I retreated to the coffee room, where we laughed ourselves silly. It wouldn't surprise me if my victim is *still* working on it.

• • •

Feeling listless? This bogus announcement, which appeared in the San Diego Police Department's newsletter, *Up Front*, should perk you up. It's courtesy of one of San Diego's finest, who's amused with all the exquisitely intricate Department Announcements on seemingly inconsequential subjects.:

Department Announcement

All Divisions and Units are requested to compile a Master List of all lists maintained by your division or unit. Please make sure to check the Master List against all other lists maintained by all other units. We need to know which division or unit maintains the most detailed lists. Please prepare a list of these divisional lists, in descending order, and forward that list to the Chief's Office. List only those divisions or units that have lists. Please compile a separate list of units or divisions that do not make lists and attach this list to the Master Descending Unit List . . . Additionally, please list the division or unit lieutenants who have no lists. List those lieutenants on a separate memorandum and forward immediately to the Internal Affairs Unit, attention List Investigation Detail.

• • •

There's no end to the shenanigans of some oversexed citizens. In late 1994 an amorous young man was arrested and charged with stealing a condom-vending machine — and its entire contents — from a rest room in Waterford, Michigan.

"He must have been anticipating a big weekend," remarked arresting officer John Grimm.

• • •

Which reminds me . . .

Communications officer Fred Sauve, of the Ontario Provincial Police in North Bay, reminisces about a prank he pulled a few years ago when he was stationed up the line in Haileybury:

One Saturday morning I received a call from the manager of a downtown hotel reporting that the night before, somebody had stolen the prophylactic vending machine from the men's room. I got on the microphone immediately and advised Constable Cliff Hallworth to proceed directly to the hotel and "see the manager about a safe job."

When Cliff arrived at the hotel he found the manager and several other people standing in the lobby. Noticing that the police had arrived, everyone's attention turned to Cliff. With a stern look of concern on his face, he asked the inevitable question: "Where's the safe?" Everyone present broke into laughter.

After learning what had actually happened, Hallworth returned to the detachment and chased me around the office, billy club in hand. Since I'm considerably younger than Cliff, he never did catch me. Eventually we sat down and had a good laugh.

• • •

Now to Springwood, New South Wales, Australia, where Constable John Stuckey tells us about a gripping adventure he had a few years ago.

Greenies and Paduspadukes

In July 1991 members of the New South Wales Police Service were sent to the Chaelundi State Forest in the northern part of the state of New South Wales, where a protest site had been developed by "greenies" demonstrating against the logging of trees in that forest. I was stationed at nearby Lismore and was sent to the Chaelundi site as one of three members of the Police Rescue Squad.

Our duties at the protest site included clearing the logging tracks of greenies so that the forestry workers could move out the logs. On arrival each morning at the protest site the police found greenies buried to their necks in the road, greenies chained to forestry equipment, trenches in the roadway, pyramids constructed of wood (some twenty feet tall) with greenies chained to them in different fashions, and anything else the greenies could think of to disrupt the progress of forestry workers.

The greenies were rather well behaved and quite peaceful. There were really only about ten fair-dinkum [genuine] greenies, and the other two hundred or so were only hangers-on with very little intelligence or understanding of the protest.

On arrival one morning we found an old van without any wheels parked on the roadway. It was painted in natural rainforest scenes, with animals, trees, and shrubs aplenty. We had instructions to move the van without causing too much damage to it or the surrounding environment. This proved a little difficult, so it gave some of the police time to think a bit.

Most of the greenies present were rather dumb and easily convinced, as we were about to find out. When we were moving the van from the road, a couple of greenies came up to us and started to talk. One of the police pushing the van became friendly with a particular greenie, and a trust was formed between the two. Few of the greenies ever spoke with us, and on the occasions when they did it was an attempt to find out our strategies. An opportunity to make fools out of these people was too good to miss.

Over lunch, a couple of policemen got their heads together and invented an animal called the "paduspaduke," which we decided looked very much like a ringtail possum. "Paduspaduke" was basically derived from the saying "Put up your dukes," but made a great name for a variety of possum. The connection between the two was made because there was a ringtail possum painted on the van that we had shifted.

After lunch, the police officer continued his conversations with his newfound friend, confiding that he was very much against the logging of the forest and adding that he was there only because of his job. He further confided that he believed that the possum painted on the van was a rare and endangered, believed-to-be-extinct paduspaduke possum.

The greenie tried to convince our officer that it was a run-of-the-mill ringtail possum, painted by one of the artistic greenies the night before, minutes after he'd seen one of the creatures. As much as our officer hated doing it, he felt obliged to convince his trusted greenie that this particular possum was the paduspaduke, and if one was seen the night before, why, this would provide real evidence to support the contention of the greenies that the logging had to be stopped. After about fifteen minutes of convincing, the greenie took the bait — hook, line, and sinker.

As the greenie ran off with a smile on his face and a twinkle in his eye, we thought the matter would be over, just another idiot greenie gone off half-cocked. We were sure that one of the fair-dinkum protesters would tell him of the joke and point out that he was the brunt of it.

Upon our arrival the next morning, we were greeted by banners and signs made by the greenies, depicting the theme of today's protest commotion — the rare and endangered paduspaduke. There were pictures of the paduspaduke everywhere, poems about the paduspaduke, all sorts of information about the habits and habitat of the paduspaduke, and the air was filled with chants pertaining to the paduspaduke. The greenies, even the fair-dinkum ones, had obviously spent a lot of time making the banners and signs for an animal that existed only in their minds.

We laughed and joked about it, but never told the greenies the real story. In many homes throughout New South Wales, many precious souvenirs have been preserved for posterity, marvellous memorabilia that proclaims the existence of the very rare, very endangered, and very extinct, paduspaduke.

• • •

Constable Jack MacNeill of the Charlottetown, Prince Edward Island, detachment of the RCMP marvels at the mischievous exploits of a certain madcap Mountie who's well known in his neck of the woods. To protect the guilty, and possibly to prevent a lynching, I've given this incurable practical joker the phoney name of Stan Smith. Here's Jack MacNeill to tell one of the tamer stories about his devilish, fun-loving colleague:

On one occasion, in rural P.E.I., Constable Stan Smith was fingerprinting a local chap who'd been charged with a minor crime, and in the process of completing the "fingerprint subject data form" he asked him to state his date and place of birth, next of kin, and penis size.

"*What?*" exclaimed the accused. Smith assured him the authorities required such information, and the man said, "Well, I don't have it." Smith sent him into the washroom with a ruler.

When the prisoner exited the privy, he was clutching the ruler and firmly holding his thumb on one of the increments of the stick in much the same way an amateur carpenter might. He then showed the officer how he measured up. Not to let the poor guy off the hook, the member (no pun intended) stated, "Gee, this is in centimetres. I need to know how long it is in inches. Please go into the adjoining office and ask one of the ladies what the conversion would be."

So, with ruler in hand once again, the poor fellow trudged into the office and asked the female clerks to give him the conversion figure, and with straight faces they provided him with the required information.

Reluctant to let a good gag get away prematurely, Constable Smith, pen poised to record the reply, asked the man quaintly, "Was the measurement taken at full strength or in a more relaxed mode?"

"Soft, of course," was the terse and rapid reply.

4

OOPS!

When I make a mistake, it's a beaut!
— Fiorello La Guardia

As you probably guessed right off the bat, this chapter is all about blunders and bloopers in the weird and wacky world of cops.

All right, guards, bring in the clowns.

———————

A policewoman named Justine Adamek, who serves with the Australian Federal Police in Canberra, wrote to me and snitched on a couple of her colleagues:

Every police officer must have worked a night shift at some stage or other, and therefore they can probably relate to this. On night shift, to stay awake, you drive around aimlessly, remembering to swap drivers every now and then. The passenger usually dozes off, so you have to prod him to wake him up.

One night, after a particularly tiring and slow shift, two colleagues of mine were returning to the police station. It was about 6:00 a.m., the sun had fully risen, and a number of the city's early birds were heading off to work. My colleagues were only one block from the station when they had to stop at a red light. The passenger was dozing, a slight snore emitting from his nasal passages. The light seemed to stay red an awfully long time.

Meanwhile, the rest of the night shift had returned to the station and were wondering where the other car was. They called the officers on the radio — no answer. After a while they decided to go and look for them. They didn't have far to go. There they were, in a fully marked police car, heads back, mouths open, dead to the world in front of a green light. Confused citizens were pulling out around them, too scared to honk their horns to wake them up!

• • •

Our raconteur from Lemoore, California, Detective Terry L. Davis, whom you met earlier, has a far more moving story to relate. Terry sent this communique from the traffic front:

The owner of a gas station called us about 5:00 a.m. one day to suggest that we check on one of our policemen, who was at that very moment behind the wheel of his cruiser, chin on chest, brake lights on, vehicle stopped in the left-turn lane. It was just starting to get light and there wasn't any traffic anywhere. The officer had stopped and, while waiting for the left-turn light to change, fell into an extremely deep sleep.

So, naturally, we engineered a lesson. Two of us drove past his cruiser at a fair clip with lights and siren turned on just as we reached the car. He awoke suddenly and shit his pants.

• • •

The foregoing reminded Terry of another tale:

I once had a sergeant who felt he had to play "big bad cop" every now and then to feel worthy of the badge. I had arrested a couple of kids for being drunk in a public place. One was real slow getting out of the car — he moved his feet out but sat on the edge of the bench seat, his head between his knees.

The sergeant decided I wasn't being assertive enough, so he grabbed the kid and jerked him out of the car. The youngster threw up all over the sergeant. There is justice, sometimes.

• • •

Ron Berry, of Chatsworth, Ontario, preserved this pip for posterity:

When I served with the Ontario Provincial Police in Port Credit, I received a commendation for work I did on a raid. Being new on the job, I was proud of the letter, sent by the commander of the Snelgrove detachment. I removed the letter from the lunch-room bulletin board and proceeded to the radio room to make a copy.

The dispatcher was watching me line up the document in the slot and pressing the button. I watched the document disappear into what I thought was a noisy copier. The look on my face made the radio operator fall off his chair, with tears streaming down his face from laughing so hard. The document came out the other side in thin, neat little strips.

The next day the staff sergeant seemed annoyed that I would take a document off the bulletin board, and he informed me that I had to replace it. I was ordered to get another copy from Snelgrove and tell them *why* I needed another copy, which made me feel even dumber. Everyone had a good laugh.

• • •

Ron returns with another yarn:

A few years ago an OPP officer — not me! — was patrolling Highway 401 when he stopped a speeder. As the officer exited the patrol car, the speeder took off.

In his excitement, the officer opened the back door of his car — and closed it — while trying to get the licence number and make of the escaping vehicle.

Well, there he sat, accidentally locked in the back of his cruiser with no way to get out or call for assistance because of the screen between the seats. Other officers made funny remarks over his radio and laughed as they drove by. Eventually they let him out.

• • •

One of the perks of police work is that officers sometimes chance upon or get summoned to scenes of great hilarity, often with little for them to do but keep an eye on things and enjoy the entertainment.

During a stroll in Regent's Park, London, England, one day in 1976, Dr. Brian Richards had occasion to deal with a serious medical situation that also had the earmarks — and lipstick marks — of a future divorce case.

In the back seat of a sports car lay a nearly naked bloke who, a few moments earlier, had slipped a disc whilst writhing in esctasy with his girlfriend. Now he was writhing in agony, and his partner had been trying in vain to escape and get help. All she'd managed to do was jam a foot against the horn, and the honking caught the attention of Dr. Richards and a bobby on his beat.

The bobby called for assistance, and soon an ambulance driver, a fireman, and a mob of gawkers were encircling the car.

91

"You won't get them out," declared the fireman, who, wielding one of the tools of his trade, began to cut the back off the sports car.

As he laboured away, two neighbourhood women started serving the trapped pair hot tea through a window of the shrinking vehicle.

"It was like the Blitz," one of them chirped later.

In due course, lover boy was transferred to an ambulance. The driver told the girlfriend, "Don't worry, he'll soon be all right."

"The hell with him," she snapped. "I'm worried about how to tell my husband what happened to his bloody car!"

• • •

Several years ago the San Diego Police Department newsletter, *Up Front,* carried this story about a copper who'd made quite a splash:

It was a dark and stormless night when Steve Molnar and Chris Smith responded to a prowler call. While checking the back yard, Steve stepped over a small retaining wall . . . and into the deep end of a swimming pool. Fortunately Steve can swim and was able to extricate himself from his predicament without assistance, since his partner was busy rolling on the ground laughing.

• • •

In this hectic old world it cuts down considerably on chaos and confusion if you know *who* you are, *where* you are, and *what* you're supposed to be doing.

A few years ago, the aforementioned *Up Front* carried this amusing little item:

Communications phone dispatchers watched a pursuit right downstairs in the police parking lot. One citizen vehicle was pursuing another, hitting the bumper of the vehicle ahead. After watching for a minute, one of the dispatchers called out, "Quick, call 911." Then they realized they *were* 911 and soon learned that the frequency-4 dispatcher had already assigned the call.

• • •

In January 1995 in Coventry, England, nine British police officers on a narcotics raid failed to reach their target after they squeezed into an elevator made for eight — causing the lift to grind to a halt.

The police were trapped in the elevator for forty-five minutes before their cries for help were heard, a London newspaper reported.

A resident of the apartment building where this happened told the captive coppers he was going to get the police, and they shouted, "We *are* the bloody police — get the fire brigade!"

• • •

Laughter sometimes erupts in extremely sad situations, even a death. Just ask Kenneth A. MacKenzie, of Hastings, Victoria, Australia. Ken, a senior detective in the Criminal Investigation Bureau of the Victoria state police, has encountered this sort of phenomenon numerous times in his thirty years as a cop. He particularly recollects a tear-splashed meeting that swiftly degenerated into slapstick:

The division van crew received word to attend a code 33 (dead body) in a block of flats and were informed that the "ambos" (ambulance men) were also on their way. On arrival, police found the deceased in a first-floor flat. He'd been dead for some time.

One officer went out onto the second-floor landing to wait for the ambos. When they arrived, one of the ambos, employing sign language, asked the officer about the state of the man's health. He extended his right arm with thumb pointing upwards (meaning, "Is he alive?") and then with thumb pointing downwards ("Is he dead?"). The officer, not completely conversant with this type of communication, replied by extending his right arm with thumb pointing upwards (which to *him* meant, "He's up here on the first floor.")

The ambos leapt into action, grabbing their many thousands of dollars' worth of lifesaving equipment from the truck and rushing to the dead man's assistance. Unfortunately the ambo carrying most of the equipment dashed across the front yard, where, failing to see the neatly pruned rosebush, he wound up spreadeagled amongst the bush and his lifesaving equipment.

After much swearing about his injured knee (poking through a large hole in his trousers), he gathered up his equipment and ran to the deceased's aid. At this point he completely lost the plot as he spent a great deal of time and energy trying to revive the dead man, much to the mirth of his offsider and the van crew.

The ambo was not seen at work (certainly not at the police station) for the next three days due to a "sickie" (sick days owed and claimed). It is still being debated whether he needed the time off to (a) allow his injured knee to mend, (b) mend his torn trousers, or (c) mend the huge dent in his pride.

• • •

Another Australian, Athol J. Montague, wrote to tell me about a horrible mess he once got into while trying to perform the hazardous duties of an Ambo. Athol is a veteran of twenty-six years with the Mortuary Ambulance Service of the police force in Launceston, a city in northern Tasmania:

I was sent to a sudden death in a suburb of Launceston and was met by a young officer fresh out of the police academy. We went to the bedroom where an elderly woman had passed away. The family wished to remain in the room to see Mother carried out in the most dignified manner.

The young constable elected to lift the feet end and left the rest to me, and I soon found out I was lifting the lot. So to get a better crack at the lift, I moved closer to the bed, placing my feet far apart, and of all places I could have put my right foot I had to stick it smack into the "family porcelain," which was full to the brim at the time.

To add to my embarrassment, my foot was wedged between the pot and the bedpost, and the more I tried to shake the stuff off my foot the worse the mess became. Naturally the family was not amused. This story found its way to the police academy in southern Tasmania, and each bunch of recruits to come to the north of the state all seem to know about it and watch their step when attending sudden deaths."

• • •

Here's another humorous tale sent by Scotland Yard veteran Hughie Brown, whom you met in chapter three.

A Case of Trespass

It was the early hours of the morning, and it had been a very quiet night to this point. Nothing very much going on anywhere in the Metropolitan Police district. Then a call came in from the information room stating that an alarm had been triggered in Park Village West, a wealthy area by any account, and that the suspect was still on the premises. It took only moments to realize that the property belonged to a lord and lady. Like all good cops, we jumped into any vehicle available and headed for the area, whilst on the way we coordinated over the radio who would take the front and who would take the rear. We would get these B & E merchants, don't you worry!

I arrived at the front of the building about the same time as the "area car." This vehicle has what is known as a seek-and-search lamp, one of those portable high-powered jobs that light up a large area. The area-car driver was a Scotsman, whose name was, naturally, Jock. He picked up the lamp and joined me as we approached the front door.

We spoke to the occupants, who were waiting for us, and they said that they heard someone try to enter the rear of the building through the French windows and that they were now somewhere in the garden at the rear and must still be there as it had been only a minute since the alarm was tripped. We radioed the guys at the rear and we all converged on the garden. It was terraced, and the bushes and trees provided a good hiding place for anyone. It was pitch-black — no garden lights, just a ray of light from the house to illuminate the patio deck. And all that did was create a silhouette as you looked back.

The lady was walking very quietly alongside us, advising us of the pitfalls in the garden. Not a sound could be heard except the crunching of leaves and twigs underfoot. Then it happened. Jock whispered, "I see him!" We froze. The lady was right behind us, looking eagerly in the direction Jock was indicating. I saw nothing, but was willing to be guided by better eyes than my own. In the firm tradition of the Metropolitan Police, Jock said, "Come on out, buddy. I can see you!" No movement at all, just an icy silence. In a slightly lowered voice, Jock snarled, "Come on out. We know you're there. This is the last warning!"

The silence that followed was getting to me. I couldn't see a bloody thing and was ready to chase in any direction. Jock had had enough. He raised the seek-and-search lamp and plastered light all over the trespasser.

It was a life-size statue of a Greek discus thrower.

• • •

You never know what's going to happen these days, do you? Consider this dispatch from Jennifer M. Kelly, of Dublin, Ireland:

One day, about twenty years ago, I opened my second-floor hair salon at 8:40 a.m., only to discover that for the umpteenth time

I was the victim of a break-in, carried out to gain access to the tobacconist's shop below. Broken glass, ripped floor covering, floorboards uprooted — an absolute mess. I phoned the police immediately and was told that the detectives were on their way and not to touch or disturb anything so that, hopefully, fingerprints could be taken. The salon was getting busy, and we were trying to cope by working around all the debris. And we kept wondering what was keeping the detectives.

About 10:30 a.m. a sergeant called from the police station and asked if the detectives had arrived, and I told him that there had been no sign of them yet. The sergeant said that was rather strange as they had left the station at 8:50 a.m. to come straight to my salon, a mere three minutes away.

At around 11:30 a.m. the sergeant rang again, and I told him the detectives still hadn't shown up. He sounded very puzzled and said, "It looks like we've lost them." At this stage I started to glance around the salon, suspecting that this whole thing was a setup and that I was a victim of the TV show *Candid Camera*. Detectives lost within a mile of their station? Come on!

Around lunchtime we heard a helicopter overhead several times, and as I'm near Dublin Airport I assumed there was something happening, some sort of event. Clients who came in during the afternoon were talking about an armed holdup at a nearby Cash and Carry, where staff were being held hostage.

The detectives finally arrived at 5:30 p.m. They apologized for the long delay and explained that they'd been held up — literally! On their way to my salon they received radio instructions from police headquarters to proceed to the Cash and Carry, where they were held hostage for the day.

• • •

Officer Brett Blacker, of Anne Arundle County Police Department, Millersville, Maryland, shudders when he thinks of a scary experience he had a few years ago:

It was near Halloween 1992, and I was working the three-to-eleven shift with a reserve officer riding along with me. At about 10 p.m. I was advised by my dispatcher that there was a possible prowler at a certain address. The call had come from a thirteen-year-old girl who was baby-sitting.

When we arrived we spoke to the girl, who said she thought someone was in the garage. So we went to check things out.

The garage door was open. After a couple of quick scans of the interior with my flashlight, I noticed a set of stairs leading to a loft. As I flashed my light up into the open area, I spotted a leg near the opening. It was wearing blue jeans and a tennis shoe. I drew my gun and pointed it at him, and my reserve radioed in and stated that I had a subject hiding in the garage.

Backup cruisers and a K-9 officer and dog were instructed to proceed directly to the scene, and meanwhile I kept telling the subject to raise his hands and slowly descend the stairs.

The subject did not respond, react, or even move. I considered going up the stairs, but figured that would be stupid. I again gave some commands and he still didn't move. I thought something wasn't right, so I decided to go up and check.

Carefully I climbed almost to the top. My plan was to reach up and grab the subject's leg and pull him down through the opening while the reserve covered me. I reached up and grabbed, only to feel the leg crinkle and crumble. I saw straw and hay sticking out of the end of his pants by his ankle.

I pulled anyway and down came the leg of a stuffed scarecrow that I later learned was stored there to be put out at Halloween. I tried in vain to dream up a way to explain this on the radio. I didn't hear the end of it for days, and now I'm the one called whenever a rogue scarecrow is on the loose.

• • •

Looking back on his lengthy career as a cop, Mike DiMiceli of Citrus Heights, California, has mirthful memories galore, which he fires off in his unique terse style:

Three a.m., warm summer night, patrol officer cruising with the windows down on a quiet residential street. He hears glass breaking and knows a window-smash burglar has just started at the clothing store in the next block. He arrives, sees no one, and waits a moment for his backup. The burglars must still be inside.

Taking their shotguns, both officers enter the store, splitting up to search. One officer turns a corner and confronts a man, standing in the corner, aiming a long gun at him. In self-defence, the officer fires the shotgun . . . and a full-length mirror is destroyed.

• • •

Mike returns for an encore:

Early morning, quiet, the young officer walks an alley on his new beat. The sergeant has told him to check the security of the stores as a way to learn the job and the beat. Keys in his pocket, walking close to the building, gun out because he's a little nervous, the officer intently scans the darkness ahead in the alley. Behind him, suddenly a big noise startles him. The officer turns and, quickly aiming, fires once. The air compressor is fatally wounded and dies with a great hiss.

• • •

Constable Andrew Maksymchuk, of the Ontario Provincial Police in Sudbury, Ontario, files this enlightened dispatch:

A few years ago, as team leader of the OPP Tactics and Rescue Unit, I was assigned to check a building for a dangerous and possibly armed suspect. Under cover of darkness, I directed my team members to strategic positions around the structure. Believing the culprit to be on the roof and hoping to surprise him, I decided to illuminate the roof by having a team member shine his flashlight in that direction on my command.

At just the right moment I whispered to the designated officer, "Throw a light on the roof." I realized my poor choice of words when I watched him switch on the flashlight and hurl it through the air towards the top of the building.

• • •

Superintendent Gary Crowell, of Peel Regional Police in Brampton, Ontario, recalls a hair-raising experience he had one night when he'd been a cop for a paltry three years.

Watch Out! He's on the Roof!

It was three days before Christmas and I was working the grave-yard shift, having started at 11:00 p.m. It was somewhat of a stormy night, but there were few calls for service. Most people were home in bed after a busy day of shopping and preparing for the upcoming holidays.

Just after midnight two officers were dispatched to a domestic call in what was usually a quiet neighbourhood. The woman caller stated that after downing numerous drinks her husband had started throwing things around the house. She added that although he had not harmed her, she was afraid for her safety. She was asked if there were any firearms in the house and she said yes. Her husband was an avid hunter and had several rifles. While not intending to go to the residence, I decided to slide over that way just in case. A short time later I was officially dispatched to the scene.

The dispatcher advised of a second call from the woman, who was now frantic because her husband had threatened to kill her for having called the police. He further warned that he'd "kill the cops" if they came near him, then he ran outside. She wasn't sure if he had any firearms with him when he left.

The first two officers said they'd park down the street and approach on foot. I was asked to approach the house through the back yard. I did so by driving to a street that ran parallel and then cutting through the adjoining yard. I was on the lookout for someone who might be watching for me. I was also very cautious as I climbed over a wire fence and entered the couple's back yard. I stopped for a few moments and listened intently for anything that might alert me to what was happening. Though we were considered a modern police force at that time, we lacked personal radios for each patrol officer. The sergeants were the only ones to carry them.

It was then that I spotted him on the roof of his house. He was crouching and appeared to be studying the front yard. I watched intently and saw him move slightly as the wind whipped up some snow around me, adding to the chill I already felt. I could only watch him and make sure he wasn't going to be a threat to the other officers. Did he have a gun? I couldn't see for sure, and I moved closer, being careful not to give myself away, when again he moved. I was more concerned now that he might have a gun, and that he had it pointed at the unsuspecting officers. I felt helpless, not being able to warn them.

For only the second time in my career, I drew my revolver and pointed it to the roof of the house. I felt sure that, for the first time, I would have to use it. There was another gust of wind and the figure moved again suddenly. I determined I had to do something. I yelled with all the voice I could muster, ordering the individual not to move and advising him that I was a police officer.

I felt he'd heard me and knew he should do as I'd asked, for he didn't even turn in my direction. I then yelled my second command, telling him to slowly stand up and raise his arms so that I could see them. No response to my verbal direction. Again I yelled my orders to him and once again nothing. At this time I noticed the other two officers running into the back yard, and I heard them calling my name. I told them to be careful and pointed to the suspect on the roof.

It took more than a few seconds for reality to set in. What

made it harder was the uncontrollable laughter that came from the two officers, who were now at my side. How could these two guys be laughing when I'd just saved their lives? What do you mean that I nearly shot St. Nick?

Between bouts of laughter, it was explained to me that the figure I'd so carefully placed under surveillance was not the runaway husband but a wooden Santa Claus mounted on the roof. When I walked to the front of the house I could easily make out the form of Santa, illuminated faintly by the streetlight. The spotlight used to accentuate his form had been turned off hours earlier. As for the husband, he'd casually approached the officers and surrendered shortly after they'd arrived.

One can imagine what the next few shifts were like for me. I was actually naive enough to think that, after several pleas for silence and offers to buy coffee for the next month, word of this fiasco would not get out. For a good long time I was the brunt of many a joke about how close I came to spoiling Christmas for the children of the world.

• • •

My eagle-eyed eldest son, Michael John MacDonald, who lives in Sydney, Australia, recently latched onto a real humdinger.

According to the newspaper clipping Michael sent me, the early evening of September 24, 1994, provided some memorable moments for residents of Sydney's east-end Dover Heights. Responding to reports that a lone gunman had "laid siege" to a redbrick house on the corner of Blake and Napier streets, thirty police officers suddenly appeared out of nowhere and swiftly sealed off a radius of 150 metres around the building.

Eighteen-year-old Ben McQueen was in his bedroom upstairs when the police swooped down on the neighbourhood at about 6:30 p.m.

"I looked out the window and thought, 'This is not normal,'"

Ben told reporters. "There were about twenty or thirty cops surrounding the house. I looked down to where my father's car was parked, and there were four police officers crouched behind it. And there were more across the road!

"They yelled for us to come out with our hands up," said Ben, who was in the house with his father. "When I went around to the back door they said there was a gunman crouched out front with a pistol aimed at the door."

Then Ben smiled and passed on some rather important information. The gunman that locals had spotted in front of Ben's home was really a life-size cardboard cutout of pistol-toting movie star Eddie Murphy, used internationally in the promotion of his latest film, *Beverly Hills Cop III*. Ben had bought it in a video store and had absentmindedly left it sitting beside the front door of the house.

"Bloody hell!" one of the flabbergasted coppers remarked.

• • •

A now-deceased sergeant of detectives in Toronto, Ontario, used to love to tell this story. His son typed it up, just the way Dad always related it:

We were called to assist a lady who, it seemed, had locked herself out of her car. She was distraught and very embarrassed. She couldn't explain how she had done it, but somehow she had put her car key in a parking-meter lock, and there it stuck! With some fiddling my partner extricated the key and she drove away, very relieved.

"Women!" I said. "How dumb can they be? Give a woman a key and you can bet she'll lose it!"

We returned to our cruiser, which we had left running, parked in a bus-loading zone.

The doors were locked.

• • •

To err is human, to forgive divine — right?

In 1993 a constable in the state of Victoria, Australia, wrote this letter to a police magazine:

Not long after leaving the police academy, I was working the station car with another junior member. A nearby van crew suddenly came up on the air asking for assistance.

First to arrive at the scene, we found the police van parked in the centre of the road with its headlights on, dazzling us. We pulled into the curb as the van started to drive off.

Imagine our surprise as we watched the van drive past with a constable hanging on to the driver's door and another clinging to the bonnet on the passenger's side! It was obvious, even to this novice, that things weren't going quite to plan.

After unceremoniously dumping its two hangers-on, the police van sped off.

With many units responding to the call, the crook was captured a couple of blocks away after he crashed the van.

Result? One written-off van, one subdued crook — and two policemen who would never again leave the keys in the ignition.

• • •

Here's a beaut from James E. Crawford, of Scarborough, Ontario:

One day in 1993 I drove my wife to a store near the corner of Bay and Bloor streets in downtown Toronto and then went looking for a parking spot, no easy task in that area. I was fortunate to find one three blocks away, and as I walked back to the store I came to the Bay-Bloor intersection again and had a fascinating upclose look at a policeman preparing a parking ticket.

The officer had a foot up on the bumper of a car, but it was obvious he was making out the ticket for the little sports car behind him. I was close enough to notice that he'd written down only the date. He was looking around, searching for a landmark or a street number, or anything else that would fix the location of the parking violation, when the little vehicle smoothly and quietly drove away. When the officer finally turned around the look on his face was priceless!

• • •

Kaye Baker, a registered nurse in Bongaree, Queensland, Australia, files this amusing but confusing report of a chaotic situation she was involved in while working in a psychiatric admissions ward:

Police brought in an extremely noisy and violent patient — there was a lot of struggling going on — and my charge nurse told me to try to remove his black-laced shoes in order to prevent a few kicks. I'm only five feet tall and I needed help in carrying out this direction.

Before long several staff members, myself included, were rolling around on the floor, trying to remove the man's shoes. I tugged and pulled for ages before coming up with a pair of shoes. After a few minutes the patient quieted down and the staff members all stood up, as did the patient.

Just then a large male staff member said, "Okay, who took off my shoes?"

I stood there, meekly holding a colleague's shoes. We all roared when we saw that the patient was still wearing his.

• • •

J.R. Richards, of Brecon, Powys, Wales, served from 1955 to 1985 with Scotland Yard, climbing all the way from constable to chief superintendent. Mr. Richards kindly sent me a batch of his funniest police recollections. The following one's pretty hairy:

In 1964 I was on an early-morning drug raid of a house in north London. We forced the front door, and as we entered, several occupants fled via the back of the house onto the overhead electric rail system at the bottom of the garden. I chased one man up the line and eventually tackled him. We struggled and rolled about and he almost broke free — so I took hold of his very long hair.

The man pulled away from me and I was left holding all his hair in my hand. I thought I'd scalped him and then realized it was a wig! The lighting was quite good and I saw this bare-headed man running away and shouting, "Me hair, me hair!" The bloke got clean away on me.

• • •

Toronto criminal lawyer Robert B. McGee tells a great yarn about his longtime friend Bill McCormack, who recently retired as chief of the Metropolitan Toronto Police Force.

"About thirty years ago," McGee begins, "young Constable McCormack and his usual partner, Constable Kevin Boyd, now deceased, were detailed to go to a swanky and exclusive apartment building on Avenue Road, where, in one of the apartments, there was supposed to be a big crap game or card game involving some big names from the world of organized crime. McCormack and Boyd were armed with a search warrant that mentioned the number of the apartment they were authorized to search."

McGee, who got this story from McCormack himself, says the officers decided they wouldn't knock on the door because that would alert the crooks inside and they'd get rid of a lot of the evidence while the cops were standing at the door.

No, said the rookies, surprise was essential. So they knocked down the door and rushed into the apartment with guns drawn.

There were no mobsters there, Bob McGee says, just four old ladies playing bridge. Someone had put the wrong apartment number on the search warrant. So here were two young officers who were hoping to advance in the force, and look at the situation they were in! What were they to do?

They said, "Sorry, ladies!" and made a beeline for an open window, where a fire escape took them quickly back down to Avenue Road.

• • •

Retired reporter Gwyn "Jocko" Thomas, who covered the crime beat for the *Toronto Star* for nearly six decades, tells this classic story about James P. Mackey, who served as chief of police in Metropolitan Toronto from 1958 to 1970:

On June 6, 1951, Sergeant of Detectives Jim Mackey, accompanied by Sergeant of Detectives Adolphus "Dolph" Payne, sped to the scene of a brutal murder in an unmarked police car.

In those days some of Toronto's detective cars were without radios so that the antennae needed back then wouldn't give them away in undercover work.

After scouring the murder site for clues, Mackey and Payne returned to police headquarters.

When they arrived, Mackey noticed a camera on the back seat of the car and asked Payne if it was his. Payne said he hadn't brought a camera, and then Mackey inquired, "Was there a radio in this car?"

Payne replied, "Sure. Don't you remember the dispatcher giving us a report of the murder?"

Payne then checked the dashboard and said, "Oh, my God, there's no radio!" Then the light flashed. As an old hand in the car-theft squad, Payne knew there were General Motors cars back then whose keys would fit many other cars of similar model.

Payne rushed to the interdepartment phone in the garage and asked the dispatcher if there were any reports of a car being stolen near the murder scene. The dispatcher said a man was on the line at that very moment reporting his car stolen.

"Tell him to stay," Payne instructed the dispatcher. "We'll be right there. We've got his car."

The detectives returned the "stolen" car and found their own car still standing where they'd left it, right next to where the other vehicle had been.

Till the day he died, many years later, Dolph Payne thoroughly enjoyed needling his good friend Jim Mackey about his brief career in crime.

• • •

One of Jocko's favourite yarns concerns a veteran Toronto policeman who was frequently and intensely preoccupied:

Inspector Bob Davie, a Scot with old-world charm, was in charge of Number 1 station, that ancient and historic structure on Court Street, which in early days was the location of the police switchboard.

Bob was the absentminded professor of the police force. He was often seen walking slowly around the downtown looking at cornerstones of old buildings, and he could tell you from memory the month and year buildings were erected.

One day Bob was leaving for a meeting at the King Edward Hotel, just down the street from Number 1 station. In those days, as is the case today, inspectors didn't usually have to wear uniforms.

But Bob had on his uniform for something that required it and then hustled back to his office to change into civvies. As he walked past the front desk towards the door, he told the station duty officer where he could be reached at the King Eddy. As he turned to walk out the door, the horrified duty officer shouted, "*Inspector, your pants!*"

Sure enough, Bob had forgotten to pull them on. In minutes, he would have been on King Street in his underwear. It was a warm summer day, and the speculation at the station was that

Bob wouldn't have known he was pantless until told.

• • •

Staff sergeant Michael McGinn of the Timmins, Ontario, police force, chortles whenever he recalls this story:

This incident happened in the summer of 1989, when I was a constable. The other officer involved was Constable Bryan Latham, a six-foot-five fellow who's a teddy bear by nature. He fancied himself quite a lady's man, and he was, but he carried a few more pounds than he should have, and all the extra weight went right to the belt line. He was nice and trim everywhere else except there. Of course, Bryan had to put his Sam Browne gun belt right at the highest bulge-point of his gut.

At about 1:30 a.m. one morning, Bryan and I were dispatched to a domestic dispute at a trailer park. The marital combatants were standing in the yard adjacent to their mobile home. The husband was on the street side of the picket fence and his wife on the other. They were shouting the usual insults, which led to neighbours calling the police.

Bryan and I arrived in different cruisers. Bryan stopped his car with the high beams aimed at the husband, about twenty feet away. We got out of our cars and tried to cool things down, but our efforts were to no avail. The husband, fresh out of the military, riproaring drunk, and spoiling for a fight, decided that if he was going to get locked up he might as well have a story to go along with it.

The battle started, and in the midst of the scrap the man somehow gave Bryan's Sam Browne a tug. That knocked the belt off the high point of his gut, causing gun, handcuffs, flashlight, and portable radio to fall to the ground. Trouble was, Bryan's pants also hit the dirt.

When the woman saw this six-foot-five giant, now dressed in polka-dot boxer shorts, fighting with her husband, she screamed and ran into the house. About this time I happened to notice Bryan's pants down around his ankles. I laughed so hard I was no longer of any assistance to my partner. Between the fresh cool air on his skin and the fact that he had trouble walking, plus the fact that I was incapacitated with laughter, Bryan finally noticed that he was rather exposed.

He threw up his hands and said, "Hold it! Just hold everything" The guy quit fighting and turned around to figure out where his wife had gone. Meanwhile, Bryan, who was still standing in the high beams of his cruiser with most of the neighbourhood looking on, pulled up his pants, walked back to his car, and called for assistance. We then got into the rhubarb again with, of course, the police coming out on top.

In jig time the story of the pantless policeman spread throughout northern Ontario — and it's still on the go, by all reports.

• • •

Officer Sunshine Dayton, of the Midtown South Precinct in New York City, sure has a way with words. She wrote to me recently and relived one of her first big adventures as a cop:

We graduated from the police academy two months previously and were eager for action — maybe a little too eager. We were working Peddler Unit — plainclothes, looking for trouble, five of us bopping down the street. We saw what appeared to be some dealing going on between two guys, and it seemed to be erupting into an argument. *Well.* We surrounded them, putting them up against the wall, and two of us started to frisk them.

John, a rookie who gave new meaning to the word "anxious," in the middle of doing the frisk suddenly yelled, "BINGO!" We all turned to him. Could this be the collar of all collars, the one we all would like to bring in? Had he found something so illegal that even the hairbags would be jealous? Before we completely went over the edge, John brought out the object of our questions, the *pièce de résistance*, the weapon of all weapons — a chopstick!

• • •

I recently received a letter from the widow of a man who served on the Ontario Provincial Police for thirty-five years. Here's her bizarre cops-and-robbers story from days of yore:

In 1946, a bank robbery near Windsor, Ontario, netted over $350,000 in cash and bonds — an extraordinary haul even today. One of the robbers was taken to a Montreal hospital with gunshot wounds in his back, and my husband, one of three OPP officers on the case, questioned him there. The man revealed that the money and bonds were buried in a suburb of Chicoutimi, Quebec.

Shortly thereafter all the loot was recovered, and the officers, heading back to their Toronto headquarters, had to stay overnight in a motel near Quebec City. While they were counting the money out loud that evening, the door to their room was smashed open by several Quebec Provincial Police officers with guns drawn. Next-door neighbours, thinking they were bank robbers, had called police.

• • •

It seems folks can get into fairly big trouble over almost anything these days — even a bit of harmless farting!

A few years ago, a Los Angeles policeman was suspended without pay for seven days for breaking wind in the presence of a couple of citizens he'd just arrested.

The officer pleaded that at the time in question he was suffering from stomach problems, but a police administrator ruled he was "feloniously flatulent" and said he'd passed gas to demonstrate his utter contempt for the prisoners.

A journalist quipped in print, "Our best advice to LAPD officers would be to walk softly and carry a big bottle of Maalox."

• • •

Humour sometimes crops up in situations of human misery. An anonymous RCMP officer is reminded of this as he recalls a sad but funny story a fellow Mountie, Corporal Kevin McCormack, once told him:

Two decades ago, when Kevin was a young, slim constable in rural Nova Scotia, he was called, along with two other Mounties, to the scene of an attempted suicide. An extremely overweight woman, despondent over a variety of issues, had chosen to take her life by jumping into an old abandoned well.

As it turned out, it clearly wasn't the time or the place to end it all. The well wasn't very deep, nor was it very full, and the lady was now at the bottom of the well and unable to do much except call for help.

When the Mounties arrived, it was decided that the slimmest and youngest member of the team — Constable Kevin McCormack — would be lowered into the well with a rope to facilitate the rescue.

Once he reached the bottom, Kevin was able to tie the rope around the victim and shout above for the other officers to start hauling.

Because of the victim's excessive weight and her inability to help her own cause, the members above had to pull for all they were worth and were only able to get the lady halfway up the well. However, Kevin was now underneath her and able to lend his shoulder to the cause.

At that point in the rescue operation it would have been fair to speculate that any number of things could possibly break — the rope, the weather, a person's composure. But the only thing that broke that day was a horrendous fart from the victim, hitting poor Kevin flush in the face.

5

The Tales of Noela, Delphine, and Michele

Ah yes! I remember it well.
— Frederick Lowe

Noela Anne Bamford has come a long way — from rookie police constable in Saskatoon, Saskatchewan, in the mid-1970s to executive director of the Labour Standards branch of the Saskatchewan Department of Labour twenty years later. She says she finds it difficult to determine when she stopped doing actual police work because all the government posts she's had along the way, including her present gig, have involved plenty of investigative work, vigorous enforcement of various provincial laws, and working closely with numerous police departments.

Noela sent me a couple of pieces she'd written culled from her "short but colourful career with the Saskatoon city police." I asked her for more of the same and, in fairly short order for such a busy person, she obliged with three additional amusing anecdotes. I was delighted.

Like Delphine Richards and Michele Smith, who are eagerly waiting in the wings, Noela Bamford has given each of her true tales a title.

Marching to a Different Drummer

When I was ten, my grade-five class took a trip to Regina, the capital of Saskatchewan, to participate in the rich educational opportunities the city had to offer. One of the things I will never forget about the trip was a visit to the Royal Canadian Mounted Police Academy. From that day on I wanted to be a Mountie and I immersed myself in exciting activities that would train me for that eventuality. Learning to walk stealthily, climb trees, spy on friends, write in secret code, and remember minute, seemingly useless details, were all part of the amazing repertoire of the tasks I set for myself. And as if all that weren't enough, I also started devouring reading material that had anything to do with the law, including the debates in the provincial legislature and Parliament of Canada and books that contained "almost true" stories about the RCMP.

My dreams of becoming a Mountie never bore fruit, but all my diligent preparation did pay off when I became only the second woman to join the Saskatoon police force many years later. I'd come straight out of university, from a culture of free love to a short-haired establishment where women still knew their place.

Any expectations I had about basic training were clouded somewhat by what I remembered seeing at ten. I had seen a glorious drill presentation, complete with a sea of red serge. Physical education had looked more like what we did at school; self-defence training had looked like fun; and swimming, well, everyone could swim.

The inspector was an ex-military man who prided himself on

being able to teach any raw recruit to march. We must truly have tested his patience. As long as the military has been in existence, the graduation exercises have always concluded with a march-past or drill-presentation.

For almost the entire period of basic training there were no uniforms or marching shoes ready for the women; they arrived just three days before graduation day. Physical education was at 7:30 a.m., followed by a quick march back to the police station for what seemed like a hundred hours a day of book learning, broken by an hour of drill practice.

Not one of us 1973 recruits will ever forget what happened one afternoon about a week before the graduation ceremonies were to be held. That day was crisp and cold and we marched in formation from the police station to HMCS Unicorn, where we would make use of their drill facilities. The inspector, resplendent in full uniform, met us and lined us up in formation. He gave us a lecture on remembering our places, proper etiquette, standing at attention, standing at ease, the proper way to step out, and other matters too numerous to mention. After having done this drill for several weeks already, it was an opportunity to tune out, providing you paid just enough attention so as not to turn the wrong way.

Well, maybe not quite. For some people marching comes naturally, and for others, the minute they try to concentrate on what they're doing, their arms, feet, and head take on lives of their own. One of the recruits was like that. He was eighteen years old, had a heart of gold, was as lovable as a St. Bernard puppy, and wasn't quite over the gangliness of youth. He bore the brunt of the inspector's wrath, and he was told often that if he couldn't turn the right way he could keep on marching out the door.

The rest of the troop was always left feeling angry and frustrated, and at the same time sympathetic toward our poor colleague and his failings. After one of these gruelling sessions in which no one could do anything right, the inspector called, "Company halt! About face!" He let us have it with both barrels about how we couldn't possibly become good officers if we couldn't march.

He then demonstrated how to accomplish the moves we were finding so difficult. As he slammed his foot down on the floor after his command, a change came over his face. The angry red colour drained away and a greyish hue replaced it. He had smashed his foot into the floor with such force that he'd broken his ankle.

The corporal in charge of the recruit troop took over from the inspector as the drill instructor. A week later, the march-past and drill demonstrations were cut short for the graduation exercises, and the entire troop survived unscathed.

Many years later I heard that the inspector had passed away. I think that if there is a God, the inspector must have gone to a Heaven where everyone can march in perfect formation and never miss a step.

The Streaker

I never liked working the midnight shift. Apart from the people who called about things that went bump in the night, there was little to keep our sense of humour alive or our eyes keenly focused on our work.

However, during the early 1970s, when streaking was the rage and police women weren't, a truly memorable incident occurred on one of those dreadful midnight shifts. You would think that during those days of free love and exhibitionism, streakers would not have been concerned about their modesty.

It was spring and the snow had melted, but the nights were still chilly. It was a time I remember well from university, when thoughts should have turned to exams, but bodies were desperate for summer and a break from the books. A group of university students out for a lark decided to bet one of their colleagues that he wouldn't dare streak through one of Saskatoon's fine establishments. In good fun he took up the challenge and ran through a particular tavern, much to the chagrin of some of the patrons and the utter revulsion of the owner.

The cheeky student ran out of the bar and into the arms of two policemen on patrol. If he thought life had taken a turn for the worse, it was about to get even more embarrassing. I was working the desk when we received a call from the officers stating that they would be bringing this young man in *sans vêtements*.

It was my job as desk officer to have accused persons empty their pockets so that I could catalogue and secure all their valuables. In this case the only pockets the prisoner would have were those that could be contained on his person. My staff sergeant was particularly interested in preserving my virtue and propriety and did not want me exposed to such a travesty.

We heard the car pull up in the garage and we could hear the policemen and the young man chuckling about the awkward state of affairs. The officers were laughing because they knew I was working the desk that night, while their prisoner was probably thinking that everything happening, including being taken to the police station, was just part of a riotous escapade.

To enter the booking station from the garage you had to climb a rise of five or six steps. The first officer walked up the steps beaming. Next came the accused, whose vision was shielded by the officer in front. Then the second officer brought up the rear, so to speak.

As the front officer stepped out of the way, the prisoner, for the first time, saw me and hastily tried to retreat behind the first officer, but his escape was blocked by the second officer behind him. The look on his face was one of sheer horror, and his hands did little to cover his exposed hide. At that stage, a fig leaf would have been welcome.

The staff sergeant, a very religious man and kind soul, came back and said with disgust, "I don't know what he was trying to show off — I have more to show in my little finger."

A Case Like This Would Drive Anyone Loony

It's funny how certain things stick in your mind and others you thought were indelibly engraved just vanish. One of the most heartwarming things I recall about police work is the strong sense of caring that so many people have for animals. It wasn't unusual to be called upon to quiet barking dogs or to herd deer or, in this particular instance, to catch a loon.

I grew up in a parkland area of Saskatchewan, near a lake where loons nested, but in Saskatoon and the area surrounding it one never heard of them. On this particular day, another officer and I were out patrolling in a relatively new area of the city, checking the construction sites and the new houses. In those days there were no stringent fitness requirements after one had passed through police college. My fellow officer was a little on the plump side. To say that he could run a mile may have been a slight exaggeration. He may have done it, but there would have been wings on more than his feet in the end.

A woman called us to say there was a loon in her back yard. She said that every time she tried to get near the bird it would chase her away. We arrived at the house with no greater resources than the weapons at our belts and the extraneous material that's carried in the trunk of a patrol car. We had no jackets in the car as it was already late May, nor did we have any raincoats, as it hadn't rained in weeks.

My partner obtained a box and the only problem then was how to get the loon into the box. He wouldn't hop in and we couldn't grab him and put him in. After several attempts we managed to put the box over the loon and folded the flaps inward so he couldn't flap his wings or bite us.

After what seemed like the better part of the afternoon, we managed to get the loon and box into the trunk of the patrol car. We dusted our hands, congratulated ourselves, and headed for the open prairie, where our prisoner could be released.

When we arrrived at a choice location to liberate the loon, we had a hard time trying to get him out of the trunk. He had somehow managed to right the box and with a self-satisfied expression dared us to try to move him. He wasn't prepared to give up the relative security of the box or the trunk. Carrying a large, uncontained bird in the trunk of a car is never a good idea at the best of times, but a bird intent on remaining there is a difficult challenge indeed. We finally managed to remove the bird from the trunk by very carefully upsetting the box out of the trunk.

You'd think that at this stage a seemingly healthy adult bird would have been quite content to fly away. But no, it stuck like glue to my partner, as in some ancient bonding ceremony or primaeval dance. My partner tried to chase the loon, and from my perspective, watching from behind, he did a fairly good imitation of the bird itself. But the loon kept circling so as to follow him. Around and around and around they went.

I, of course, was of little help. My sides were splitting from the intense pain caused by the guffaws that were caught in my gullet, and tears were streaming down my cheeks. My fellow officer, on the other hand, was extremely unamused.

It seemed like an eternity, but at last the bird appeared to sense that Mike was not his mother, and the fun they'd been having began to wane. He took to the sky, flying northward, never to be seen again.

Treed in Saskatoon

It was just one of those nights. It was in the fall and Saskatoon's municipal outdoor swimming pools had closed. We were looking for a runaway and had received a report that he had been seen hanging out in the area of one of the city's pools. I met the "dog-man" at the site and, to help illuminate the area, had driven my car up on the lawn, with the headlights shining through the chain-link fence at the buildings within the pool area. The dog-man had arrived before me and was already inside the compound. Trying to put a little light on the subject, I had taken a large magnifying light and was shining it at the buildings from a vantage point on the hood of the patrol car.

Most of us are equipped with intuition, a sixth sense of being watched. The hair on the back of my neck bristled and a shiver ran down my back. Was this excitement? Out of the corner of my eye I saw a slight movement. I froze. I turned off the light, but it took quite a while for my eyes to readjust to the darkness. Just as I went to lower my arm to reach for my gun, I heard it — the unmistakable sound of a large dog growling.

Cautiously I looked around. The dog-man was nowhere to be seen. Unbeknownst to me, he had managed to exit the pool area via another route and had decided to have a little fun. He knew exactly where I was, and it had been relatively easy to give the dog a command to guard. It was not so easy, however, to call the dog off once the handler, seeing my plight, was hysterically rolling on the ground.

There I was, stuck on the hood of the patrol car, held captive by one of my peers. The dog refused to give up his post, and the dog-man was laughing so hard the dog wasn't certain what to do. Every time I tried to move a little, the dog would growl, and that would start the howls of laughter all over again.

After what seemed like an eternity, the dog-man managed to regain enough composure to control his dog. Calling off the dog was not unlike being granted clemency. I suspect that if I'd been up there any longer, I would have become a permanently attached hood ornament on that car.

The Chocolate Marshmallow Heist

When I think about police work I tend to think about the great detectives of Scotland Yard, or Sherlock Holmes, or at least Columbo of television fame. I always wanted to believe that at the end of the first hour or, if pressed, the first hour and a half,

I, too, would have found the culprit and had him safely in custody. Usually things don't work out that way, but one winter's night they did.

It was the midnight shift and we'd just had a fresh fall of snow. We received a call on the police radio that a break-in was in progress at a small neighbourhood grocery store. Every available patrol car headed to that location. My partner and I walked around the building and discovered a trail of cookies leading from the store and down an adjacent alley. We thought at first it had been spillage on the way to the trash, but the cookies continued on down the alley. In the freshly fallen snow we had little difficulty following them to the rear of a house a couple of blocks away. By this time there were several police cars in the vicinity, and one of the other officers had seen a fellow climbing up a trellis to a second-floor window.

We arrived on the scene and surveyed the situation from the back yard. It seemed improbable that any crime detection could be this easy. We entered the house. Music was playing in the suite on the main floor. The second floor was in darkness, but we could hear some scurrying as we approached, then silence.

The door was locked, but it was opened at our knock by a young man rubbing his eyes as though he'd been sleeping. We searched the premises. Lying in bed in one of the bedrooms was a man in his early twenties, out of breath, red in the face, pretending to sleep, with the lingering odour of chocolate cookies on his breath. We threw off the covers and there he was in all his glory — winter jacket still stuffed with cookies and his winter boots melting snow into the sheets.

Years later, as I watched the attack of the Marshmallow Man in the movie *Ghostbusters*, I was reminded of the young man we'd tracked down with such ease. The only thing he'd stolen that night was a case of chocolate marshmallow puffs, and most of what he hadn't been able to eat he lost in his hurry to get home. The cookies we retained for evidence managed to perfume my locker for months. Yum, the sweet smell of chocolate. Or was it the sweet smell of success?

Delphine Richards is a thirty-eight-year-old former policewoman from Wales — Cysgod-Y-Castell, Dryslwyn, Carmarthen, Dyfed, Wales, to be precise. She served on the Dyfed-Powys Police Force from 1978 to 1991, the year she was operated on for a brain tumour. She recovered nicely and now works part-time as a free-lance journalist. Her husband, Heddwyn, is the area manager of a building society.

The Dyfed-Powys Police Force serves about 250,000 people in Britain's largest police territory — a triangular tract of mostly rural real estate that measures roughly 100 by 100 by 70 miles. Delphine worked exclusively in the county of Dyfed, operating out of the police station in the town of Ammanford. Her beat consisted of three villages — Brynamman, Glanamman, and Garnant — and, of course, the countryside in between.

"Those villages used to have a small police station each," Delphine told me, "but due to cuts in public spending in the 1970s these were closed. This meant that the police car was a sort of mobile police station for the time it spent in each village. The system worked quite well, as the villagers always saw the same five or six officers during a period of years and were able to approach them (or avoid them!) with some familiarity."

Delphine enjoyed her thirteen years on the force. "I liked being among the people, doing important work," she says. "It was often thrilling to be in the middle of things. You know what I mean — you're *there*, deeply involved in a situation, not read-ing about it or hearing about it later."

'Was there a lot of crime in your neck of the woods?" I asked her.

"It's a farming and coal-mining area, with lots of heavy drink-ing going on, which leads to quite a few cases of vandalism and stolen animals that the police have to try to track down," she replied. "We averaged about one murder a year, and I helped investigate five or six of them. But for the most part I was involved in minor crimes, and so were our other officers — the kinds of offences that are mentioned in my stories."

She was referring to the batch of true tales about police work in rural Wales that she'd written and sent to me. Here they are, just as Delphine presented them.

A Funny Thing Happened

It was a fine autumn evening. I was working the Sunday-evening shift (5:00 p.m. to 1:00 a.m.), and with my list of things to do consisting only of taking a simple witness statement from a very pleasant couple at their home, the evening promised to have an almost recreational quality.

I set off from the station at a leisurely driving speed to match my mood — a mood that lasted until I rounded a bend on the outskirts of the village where the couple lived. There were four or five cars stationary in the road with their drivers standing behind the open doors while the leading car inched forward, cautiously trying to avoid the attentions of a large, hairy billy goat who, at regular intervals, reared up and butted the side of the car with alarming force.

My first thought was to do a quick U-turn and vanish into the night. But too late! The occupants of the vehicles were looking at the police car with a "Here comes the cavalry" look on their faces, and I was forced to park and get out of the car. In defence of my cowardice, I have to say that I was brought up on a farm, and the size of the goat did not overly alarm me — I had seen bigger Shetland ponies, and cattle were in a completely different league. It was not even the "regimental mascot" quality of his horns and his aggressive use of them that worried me. No, it was something far more basic than that. In the autumn, the young (and even downright decrepit) goat's fancy turns to love. Unattached goats often live miles away from other unattached goats. So, in order to relay his availability to the female goat population, the male becomes possessed of an odour that, to goats, is equivalent to Chanel No. 5, but to all other living forms is highly objectionable. It is also indelible.

I walked slowly towards the billy goat, held out my hand, and tried to look confident. He gave the first car another butt for good measure, then turned to look at me. His yellow eyes half closed and he adopted a relaxed posture that a moment later I saw was also a urinating posture. Unfortunately frustrated billy goats urinate along the underneath of the belly, spraying the hair of the abdomen, chest, front legs, and beard, if the head is hanging down, with a fresh supply of Eau de Goat to ensure that opportunities are not missed.

I continued to walk up to him and quickly grabbed his beard and thrust his chin skyward. Thus encumbered, he was unable to butt me and I began to half-drag, half-lead him along to the side of the road. A friendly but cautious local resident walked behind him, making encouraging "gee-up" noises, and pointed out a nearby building plot that the goat had obviously come from. We completed the hundred yards or so at a slow walk, stopping only when the goat again urinated, this time splashing the back of my legs. By then I was breathing neat goat fumes and was fairly immune to any extra smell.

I secured the goat, under supervision of the friendly resident, who then eyed me distastefully and said, "You'd better come and wash your hands." This I did in his garden outhouse with a block of carbolic soap and a whole bottle of Dettol before I set off again. I had also sponged down my uniform with Dettol, and for five minutes the inside of the patrol car smelled like a pot-pourri that had passed its sell-by date. By the time I reached the house of the statement-makers the Eau de Goat was back.

I went into the house, apologizing profusely and explaining what had happened, but they politely said that they couldn't smell a thing. I had actually begun to believe them until their young son, with the innocence and tactlessness of youth, said, "Ugh! What's that smell?" as he walked into the lounge. I was in the kitchen.

I quickly finished taking the statement and went back to the station for another dousing in Dettol and a change of as many articles of clothing as I kept in my locker, but to no avail. The smell stayed with me until I went home and had a bath.

I had hoped that was the end of the incident, but I was to suffer two other indignities. The next morning, as I prepared to attend court, I became faintly aware that the smell was still lingering. However, I put it down to imagination until, much later, sitting in a warm courthouse, I knew I had not been mistaken. Worse still, every time the doors swung shut, circulating the air, the experience was shared by those sitting two rows behind me. It was much later in the day when I discovered that the odour was ingrained in my watch strap and I was, at last, able to be rid of it.

The final affront came some days later. One of my colleagues, spending an evening at his local tavern, had met up with the driver of one of the cars attacked by the goat. He related the tale and seemed most impressed by my action, telling the other man, "That policewoman was small, but she sure knew how to handle a billy."

Eighteen-Month Mutton

This incident occurred at Ammanford during the early 1980s. Due to an unfenced mountain road leading to the town, the knocking down and killing of farm livestock is a regular occurrence. Stan (not his real name) died a few years after retirement, and both he and this tale are remembered with great affection. Karen (also not her real name), a fully accomplished Criminal Investigation Department officer for some years, now works at a specialized CID unit in Bristol, England.

Stan was an old-fashioned sergeant. Nearing retirement, he remembered the old days in the force when discipline was stricter than it is now — and women were not a relevant part of the police service.

To add to his chagrin, Stan had a young policewoman on his shift — that is, her name appeared on his duty rota. But the number of times she had worked with his shift were few and far between. This was because the Criminal Investigation Department had taken her to assist them in a delicate case in which a female officer was needed. So Karen spent the first six months or so of her service in the comfort of the CID office.

To say that Stan disliked female officers is an understatement. To say that he had very little affection for the CID is downright perjury. So for Karen, being a member of the fairer sex and having so much contact with the CID, her career was doomed in Stan's eyes. He was praying for an opportunity to see her perform at the "sharp end," which means patrolling the street in the rain and other unpleasant tasks.

Stan thought his wish had come true one rainy Saturday afternoon. A passing motorist called in at the station to report that he had knocked down and killed a sheep on the unfenced mountain road some miles away. By the remotest chance Karen was also working with the shift that day, and Stan decided that she should record and deal with the incident.

Recording the motorist's documents at the station was no problem to her. That done, Stan, with some relish, instructed her to drive out to the scene of the accident to take measurements of the road, identify the sheep, and contact the owner to collect the carcass.

"How do I identify the sheep, Sarge?" she asked in all innocence.

Impatiently Stan explained that there should be a dye mark on the sheep's wool or, failing that, a series of holes punched through the tip of the animal's ear. Different patterns were registered to different farms.

Off she went, armed with measuring tape, accident booklet,

waterproof pen, and Stan's dark suggestion that she should not bloody return until the task was completed.

In the lashing rain she found the sheep lying at the roadside. It was immediately apparent that she would not find a dye mark because the sheep was covered in . . . whatever sheep are covered in, apart from wool, and it STANK!

Peering closely at the tip of the sheep's ear, she eventually found the pattern of holes — except that they did not make a pattern at all, whichever angle she looked at them. She considered calling Stan on the radio to ask for advice, but decided that would be an unwise move.

Then, as another drip of rainwater ran down the back of her neck, the solution presented itself to her. She had not spent all that time in the CID for nothing.

She fetched a sharp knife from the first-aid box in the patrol car and commenced to cut the ear-tip off. *Sawing* it would be a more apt word, as even the tip of the ear was gristly. With her prize in hand, she popped it into a discarded Big Mac box the previous occupant of the patrol car had abandoned there and proudly bore it back to the station.

From there on the exercise was simple — compare the ear-tip to the book of registered markings and phone the farmer to inform him that one of his sheep had departed this world and had gone to the Big Sheep Pen in the Sky.

An hour later, Stan called Karen into his office.

"You've got your bloody map references arse backwards," he told her, always mindful of his language in the presence of women. "That farmer can't find the sheep where you said it was! Get the car and show me where it is."

So, for the second time that day, Karen found herself driving onto the mountain road. They arrived at the spot, but true enough, there was no sheep. They then drove up and down the road a few times before returning to the original scene.

"It was definitely here," insisted Karen. But Stan did not seem to be listening to her. He was gazing into the middle distance, unusually silent. Eventually he said, "Does *that* sheep look familiar to you?"

Karen looked — and wished she was somewhere else. Like at the dentist's having an extraction without anaesthetic. There, on a rocky bank, was a grazing sheep — probably stone-deaf — with half its ear missing!

Karen now works permanently with the CID.

Tales of Flatfoot I

If the USA has Bigfoot, then, during the 1940s, a small village in Wales had an even greater phenomenon — Flatfoot.

Flatfoot was the village bobby, and never before or since his reign has a policeman been so unpopular with his villagers. Whatever name Flatfoot had been registered under by his mother (many say Pete Jones), there is not a villager alive now who can remember that name. He will always be just Flatfoot.

Flatfoot was a tall, heavyset man who was given his wither-shins nickname due to his propensity for sneaking up quietly on wrongdoers (and even rightdoers!) and scaring the hell out of them. During the years Flatfoot was stationed at the village of Llandyssul in West Wales, dozens of tales originated about him, many of them undoubtedly true. The first I remember was told to me by my grandfather. Grandfather and his drinking partner Glyn had spent the evening at the village tavern building up a festive spirit for Christmas, which was about a week away.

On leaving the tavern and stepping into the darkness, Glyn saw the lights of Flatfoot's bicycle heading towards them. Glyn immediately threw himself on his hands and knees in the grass verge and began searching through the grass.

"Help me look, Davey," muttered Glyn, and Grandfather, not quite sure what they were looking for, but too full of ale to much care, obliged.

The weaving light of Flatfoot's bike came to a halt beside them.

"Have you lost something, Glyn?" asked Flatfoot, who was obviously the perceptive type.

"Sixpence," came the reply.

Although in those days sixpence was not a fortune, to poorer folk like Grandfather and Glyn, its loss could not be dismissed lightly.

Flatfoot took the lamp off the handlebars of his bicycle and got down on hands and knees to help them look.

"Was it definitely here that you lost it?" asked Flatfoot after five minutes and a damp knee from kneeling in the grass.

"Yes, right here," said Glyn, who had stopped looking himself and was watching Flatfoot.

"When did you lose it?" asked Flatfoot after a few more minutes, more out of a need to make conversation than for any scientific reason.

"About last Easter!" shouted Glyn as he and Grandfather sprinted unsteadily down the road.

• • •

Tales of Flatfoot II

The time Flatfoot's patience was put to the test — and failed — was when the Romany Gypsies camped on Grandfather's field.

Every year they would spend a week or fortnight on the field, sometimes helping Grandfather with some maintenance repairs for his kindness. If there were no repairs needed, as was often the case, they would feel morally obliged to sell Grandfather a horse at a "bargain" price. Considering that the bargain usually took three or four months before it would be caught or harnessed, it *is* surprising that Grandfather did not support Flatfoot's attempts to evict them.

One such year Flatfoot stood on Grandfather's doorstep demanding that the Gypsies be moved on, as their stay was illegal. Grandfather was adamant that they be allowed to stay.

"I've got a book on law," said Grandfather, "and if you will just wait a minute while I fetch it, I would like to argue a legal point with you." (Grandfather had always fancied himself as a lawyer and could be a pain in the arse about such things!)

He strode into the house with Flatfoot following a few feet behind, then went through the kitchen and into a back room. Meanwhile, Flatfoot, arriving in the kitchen, stood his ground behind Grandmother, who was taking a rice pudding out of the fireside oven.

At that time oven gloves were not what they are today, and the heat of the pudding basin soon began to spread through the towel she had used. Knowing that she had approximately one and a half seconds to reach the table, Grandmother spun around, rice-pudding basin in hand, and collided squarely with Flatfoot, tipping most of the contents over him. With the rice and milk trickling down the uniform front, Grandmother managed to keep her response to a simple "Oops," which was considerably less colourful than Flatfoot's reply.

Incidentally, the "point of law" was never argued.

• • •

This tale, according to Delphine, happened in the mid-1980s at Llandybie, near Ammanford, Dyfed, West Wales. She says the constable's real-life name is Wyn Jenkins and he retired in 1994.

A Fishy Story

Wyn was working the evening shift one Saturday when he was flagged down by the driver of a mobile fish shop. He explained that someone had stolen some fish from his van as he made his deliveries around a housing estate.

Wyn took all the details, feeling genuinely sorry for him. In his effort to make a success of his business the man could always be seen delivering fish around many of the villages. Rarely did he have a holiday or take a day off. On Saturdays he would rise early and drive to the nearest coastal town some fifty miles away in order to meet the fishing boats coming in from the sea.

Then, fully stocked, he would spend all day and most of the evening selling and delivering the fresh fish he had bought. Petty thieves he could do without.

"Any idea who took them?" asked Wyn.

"Well, I saw two of Sam Stud's boys hanging around," he said, "but I didn't actually see them take the fish."

This came as no surprise to Wyn. Most of the petty crime in the area could be attributed to Sam Stud or his many offspring. Sam had acquired his nickname due to his reputation for fathering eleven children with his own wife and, allegedly, many more with other men's wives. Considering that Sam had a squint, a bad stutter, and several missing teeth, he was certainly no Mel Gibson, so his history as a potent sire was probably overrated.

However, Wyn did not concern himself with this and went in search of the boys. Pretty soon he saw two of Sam Stud's sons walking through the park. One of them had a paper parcel under his arm.

"What have you got under your arm?" asked Wyn.

"Hair," said Sam Junior, who had picked up a thing or two from his father.

Without further delay, Wyn got him to unwrap the parcel and saw that it contained three fish.

"Whose are these?" asked Wyn.

"Ours," said Sam Junior. "We just caught them in the river."

A reasonable explanation, thought Wyn — reasonable, that is, if the fish had been on steroids. Wyn could think of no other explanation for sea mackerel swimming fifty miles inshore to be caught!

What's in a Name?

There had been a spate of bicycle thefts on my patch. The culprit, clearly an opportunist, had an uncanny knack of being around when the owners of the bicycles, mostly teenagers, temporarily abandoned them for some other diversion. Despite parental persuasion and threats, reckless teenagers still left their bikes unattended, and inevitably the thefts continued.

My mind was on far more pleasant matters as I travelled along a woodland road outside the village one day. The sight of a boy zooming across my vision centimetres in front of the police car as he crossed from one woodland to another soon restored my concentration (not to mention my bowel efficiency) and I came to an abrupt halt.

Intent on giving the boy some earache about his lack of road safety, I followed the rough path through the woods on foot. Within a short distance I saw a roughly made shelter, and on looking inside I found the boy, his rocket-assisted bicycle, and several other bikes in various stages of being dismantled.

The boy was obviously well versed in matters of law and refused to say anything, so there was nothing to do but to ferry him back to the police station. Since he appeared to be only about fifteen, it was essential that his parents be contacted so that he could be interviewed in their presence. The only slight technical hitch was that Boy Wonder was still not talking.

Eventually, however, after persuasive interview techniques were employed, he gave his name as Jason Davies and an address some six miles away before clamming up again. As the surname Davies was shared by a majority of the Welsh population, the phone book was left on the shelf and another constable was sent to see Jason's parents. He reported back that no such person lived at the given address.

So once more I questioned Jason, who by now had decided that his name was Robert Jones and he lived somewhere else. As Jones comes a close second in the popular-surname stakes to Davies, the same constable was again sent on his quest. And again the same result was relayed back to me: "No such person living at this address."

By then I was beginning to lose patience with Jason/Robert and again asked him for his name, while reminding him — inaccurately — how long he was likely to remain at the station if he failed to give me the correct details.

With a quivering lip he said, "All right, my name's Elvis — Elvis Woolley-Dick."

That was the final straw. Forgetting "Interview of Juveniles, Part 3," and forgetting that I could be heard in the inspector's office and the Indian takeout place across the road, I let rip at Jason/Robert.

"Elvis Woolley-Dick!" I shrieked before comparing him to various waste-producing parts of the human anatomy. I questioned his ability to recognize truth, which was allied to the fact that his parents were probably unmarried. I suggested that his brain had been borrowed from a retarded gnat and was just building up nicely to the "bad cop" routine when there was a little cough from the doorway.

The station officer stood there.

"I've got a bloke on the phone," he said. "It's a Mr. Woolley-Dick, and he wants to know if we've got his son Elvis here."

• • •

The following story is a true account of the crash of a military aircraft in 1979. "Ivor's real name has been spared," Delphine says, "but records still exist with all the necessary details in case verification is required."

Ivor's Flight of Fancy

The area surrounding the small town of Lampeter in West Wales is dominated by farmland and mountainous terrain where sheep outnumber people by about two hundred to one. The sparsely manned police station in the town seldom experiences more than the most routine and mundane of crimes and incidents.

The nearby hills, home to the swooping red kite, have another impressive flyer over their summits — the fighter planes of the RAF. The peace of the Lampeter countryside in the direct line of the jets' training run through mid-Wales, is regularly shattered by Tornados and similar low-flying aircraft.

One of the police officers allocated to this rural area was Ivor. Ivor was a steady, unflappable sort. No longer a young man, he had been born in an age and an area where Welsh was most people's first language. Like his peers, he would think in Welsh before speaking in English. In the Welsh he was "one of the boys," but when speaking English he would speak slowly, clearly, and with the use of as much official jargon as he could muster. If Ivor heard a new phrase or word once, he would be eager to repeat same to emphasize his great sagacity. It was fortunate that it was someone of Ivor's calm disposition who was on duty the day a major incident occurred.

A low-flying aircraft, out on a training run, crashed into the hills outside Lampeter. Its demise could even be seen from the town.

Headquarters contacted Ivor on the radio and sent him to the scene to initiate action. Simultaneously the information given by HQ to Ivor was heard on every police radio throughout two divisions. A plane crash of any sort was an incident of great magnitude and rarity within this police area. All across the country, patrolling police officers listened to the course of events over their two-way radios.

Meanwhile, Ivor had parked his patrol car on the last stretch of road leading to the hills and walked the remaining distance to the inferno. Due to his somewhat rotund figure and the rather severe angle of the countryside, by the time he had approached the wreckage, the RAF had already arrived in helicopters and were briskly going about their business.

Ivor spoke to the man in charge, then, with an air of importance, switched on his radio to inform headquarters of the outcome.

"Go ahead, Bravo One Two," said the inspector at HQ eagerly when he heard Ivor coming through, and throughout the division, police officers strained to hear all the gory details.

"Regarding the aircraft crash at Lampeter hills," said Ivor slowly and clearly, if a little out of breath, "I have the investigation team from RAF Brawdy at the scene. There have been *no*, I repeat *no*, fatalities as the pilot appears to have ejaculated over Lampeter town."

Australian police officer Michele J. Smith has a wonderful story she's itching to tell, one that took place at — and atop — a certain fence in the big city of Adelaide, South Australia. Recently she was appointed officer in charge of her own police station at Port Germein, "a first for a woman police officer in South Australia, and maybe Australia," she says with justifiable pride. The pandemonium Michele describes herein erupted one peaceful day . . .

The Great Fence Caper

The South Australia Police Department was, and is, a bit of a dinosaur. The hierarchy clings firmly to images of Mum and wild-peach pie. In 1983 this meant that policewomen were meant to be ladies — no matter what the situation. The feminist movement and the Miss Manners brigade were clashing heads at every turn, leaving the department directors slightly dazed.

The nubile women who trained with the boys now wanted to do the same jobs as the boys. Doing the gentry's typing and wiping the noses of snotty lost children just didn't cut it anymore.

The lords upon high, however, became more addled and sat down together to ponder. The subject was complex and no consultation was sought, but finally an answer emerged. Women could actually do real police work maybe, but just to be safe and to preserve the sweetness and light of all that women represented, policewomen must wear pretty skirts and ladylike dress shoes with two-inch heels. As for arms and equipment, well, "Stand next to a man, sweetie, and you'll be okay."

Unfortunately for some — and I was one — this led to some dangerous, funny, ridiculous, and sad incidents. Mine goes like this:

I was working an afternoon shift out of police headquarters in Adelaide. I looked good: trim, taut, and terrific in my very tight-fitting navy-blue A-line skirt, with one pocket just big enough for car keys and not a lot else. The skirt skimmed the knees and, as mentioned, was not very roomy. My gun and other essentials were popped into a handbag Daisy Duck would have been proud of and immediately slung into the boot of the car, until I finished work and handed it all back. Tall, dark, and cute, Bob hopped into the car with me and off we went. The world was a safer place — we were out there.

On this sunny afternoon the radio was quiet, people were happy, and we pottered along smiling at everyone. Then it happened. The West Torrens Football Club alarm had been activated, and it was thought the intruders were inside.

We raced to the location, light flashing through the five-o'clock peak-hour traffic. We made it up onto the footpath right outside the grounds. There, on South Road, with a million cars crawling past, was the object of our dash through this crush of cars and pollution. Only one thing stood in our way. A fence. A three-foot brick fence topped with six feet of cyclone mesh.

I teetered on my dainty shoes as virile young Bob muscled his way effortlessly over the fence. I gazed down at my skirt and my footwear. I gazed skywards and knew then that God was a man.

Determined to prove I was as good as any man, I strode on. I hitched my skirt slightly waistwards, and the brick part of the fence proved no match for me at all. Now, however, the fun began. I started to climb the mesh. The vehicles on South Road began to slow down. The drivers began to gawk. The horns started to beep.

I made it to the top and hitched the skirt up a little higher. The cars stopped. Who can blame them? How often does one see a blonde policewoman sitting on a fence with her skirt around her ears?

I tried to continue and begin my descent on the other side. I didn't get very far. I was stuck. (Luckily, my skirt was covering my face so no one could see how embarrassed I was!) I tugged a bit harder, but I wasn't going anywhere.

I could see dear Bob hesitating. Should he go catch the crooks or rescue this dingbat stuck on the fence? I knew Bob. He was kind, thoughtful, chivalrous, and cute. I arranged an appropriate thank-you in my head.

He chased the crooks.

My face flaming, my nether regions exposed, the car horns blaring, the offers of marriage, money, and good times coming thick and fast, I made one last effort and fell in a crumpled heap on the crooks' side of the fence. The only trouble was that part of my skirt, panty hose, and knickers stayed with the fence, waving like a banner in the breeze to the milling crowd. I arose with what dignity I had left and teetered after dear Bob and the crooks.

My story is humorous, but other women's stories from that time often were not. Gradually the women were assimilated into the police force and no longer had to endure novelty value. I tell you what, though — I never wore a skirt for patrol work again.

And the crooks?

It was a false alarm.

6

ROOKIES

You cannot create experience. You must undergo it.
— Albert Camus

One thing you can say about rookie cops is that over the years they'll have countless learning experiences that will boost their confidence and performance tremendously, and before long they'll be known as veterans. Experience is the best teacher, and as George Bernard Shaw once noted, "Everything happens to everybody sooner or later if there is time enough."

Also, while working their butts off, neophyte coppers are occasionally presented with the opportunity to laugh their guts out, too.

Superintendent Gary Crowell, of Peel Regional Police in Brampton, Ontario, chuckles whenever he recalls a particular drive he took when he was a gung-ho, freshly minted Mountie.

A Day I'll Never Forget

It was early spring 1971, and I had just finished my basic training with the RCMP in Regina, Saskatchewan. I was posted to Dartmouth, Nova Scotia, and was most eager to assume my duties as a police officer. Six months' training had been long enough, to my way of thinking, and now I was ready.

The first day and a half had been spent unpacking and establishing myself in my new home, which was in the detachment. I was one of four constables assigned to the single men's barracks, encompassed in an older, converted, ranch-style house. The rest of the time I was busy meeting the detachment personnel and bringing myself up to scratch by reading routine orders and familiarizing myself with office routine.

On the third day I was up bright and early, two hours before I was to begin my first real day of duty as a police officer. This was to the chagrin of two officers who were trying to get some well-deserved sleep. But nothing was going to stop me from preparing my uniform and equipment, not even a pillow tossed my way. Everything had to be just right. Nothing beats the RCMP for teaching a youngster what *image* is all about. At exactly 8:00 a.m., I left the barracks and entered the office — and was immediately reprimanded by the corporal for not having arrived earlier.

I paced the office floor, waiting for the go-ahead to go out on patrol by myself. I soon realized, however, that before I would be given this freedom, the corporal had a list of things he wanted me to do. This included reading recent crime reports, typing out some forms, and filing a week's worth of teletype messages. For this I needed six months' training? However, the corporal finally threw me a set of cruiser keys and assigned me the area I would be patrolling for the remainder of my shift.

I spent my first ten minutes going over my cruiser inside and out, just like the procedure stated, to assure I would be ready for whatever came my way. Or so I thought. I'll never forget the feeling that came over me as I eased the gearshift lever into reverse. Finally this was it! I was on my own! A police officer going on patrol for the first time, solo, and without a tether. This thought was quickly interrupted when I realized that the corporal was standing at the front door of the detachment, waving to get my attention.

Well, it wasn't as bad as I had first thought. He only wanted an envelope delivered to division headquarters, across the harbour in Halifax. I could handle this, and well. It was sort of on my way to the patrol area I had been assigned. Not being familiar with the Halifax area, I checked my map and quickly planned my route. Before long I crossed over the bridge (there are now two bridges) that divided the cities of Halifax and Dartmouth and spanned the famous harbour.

I cannot tell you the exhilaration I felt driving that cruiser, dressed in uniform and alone for the first time. I sat tall and erect, making sure my driving was an example for others. I was not used to the looks I got from motorists, who, when they realized who they were driving next to, quickly checked their own driving habits. This caused some to slow down and brake sharply and others to signal their every move. I smiled at this obvious and sometimes discreet compliance with the traffic laws.

To this day I will not admit, even to myself, that I was lost. I rather like to explain that I was a newcomer to the Halifax area and that I was having a good look around. I knew that my destination lay just around the next corner, or perhaps the one after that. It was then I recognized the name of one of the streets I had selected for my carefully planned trip.

As I turned onto the street I saw seven people waving at me. This was something else I was not used to as a rookie officer, yet it was an experience I enjoyed. I enjoy it to this day, not because of the recognition but because it's a reminder of the support and the respect the public generally has for the police.

This was a friendly street, indeed, because everyone seemed to wave at me as I passed. I waved back and smiled. The people in the cars even acknowledged my presence by waving, and one even gave a slight tap on his car horn so that I would not miss his greeting. Just up ahead I noticed a motorist hastily exit his vehicle, which he appeared to have abandoned right in the middle of the street. He waved frantically at me, motioning for me to stop.

This is what the six months of training had been for. Those early-morning parades, late nights studying laws, procedures, rules, and regulations. All the time spent on marching, phys ed, firearms training, and even defensive driving, came down to this — serving the public, helping someone in need, and, if necessary, putting your life on the line. Yes, this was what it was all about — finally a chance to do police work.

I stopped my cruiser and didn't even have time to get out when the man rushed to my door. I rolled the window down, at which time I expected to hear of some dastardly deed or a plea for help. Instead, he blurted out something that even the most experienced instructor had not prepared me for: "Officer, you're driving the wrong way down a one-way street!"

Although it really had not been that far, the street now seemed as long as the Trans-Canada Highway. There was no escape, no side street in which to make a quick disappearance. I was compelled to go back the way I had come and, once again, pass those same people who'd remained to see how far I would really get. I did so, only this time my face was as crimson as the tunic that I had graduated in just a week before.

• • •

Former Ontario cop Morley Lymburner, editor and publisher of a popular national police magazine called *Blue Line*, loves to reminisce about some of his scariest moments on the force. He wrote this story during a fit of nerve-wracking nostalgia.

The Rookie and the Prowler

I was a young rookie just out of police college and coupled with a training officer. This guy sized me up for the first couple of hours and realized I was keen and energetic. He started to ask me questions about the training they gave us at the college. He said he'd heard it had changed since he had his little cakewalk ten years before. I told him it was gruelling and said I was very happy to have graduated. He asked me about the physical training, and I told him it was extremely tough and had produced some of the best-conditioned officers in the entire country.

Around dusk we began to patrol an industrial area of our sector. My coach-officer told me there'd been a lot of factory break-ins lately, which police reckoned had been committed around sunset. They called the culprit the Twilight Burglar.

As we drove past a factory at the end of a cul-de-sac, my partner suddenly shouted, "There he goes! He ran down the alley! Did you see him?" Far be it for the rookie, a trained observer straight out of police college, not to see something that obvious. "Yeah, sure, I saw him," I lied.

"Okay," said my mentor, "there's no way he's getting out of the rear of that factory. You go down that side and I'll go down the other side. We've got him for sure!"

I exited the passenger side of the car and got out my flashlight. I could see what my partner meant — there was a high barbed-wire-topped fence to the rear, and there was no way that guy could get out of there. I ran to the back of the factory and shone the light across the tall grass by the high fence.

Suddenly I could hear some rustling to my left. I knew I had the guy now, and I quickly shone my light towards the ever-increasing rustling sounds. My stomach started to churn, for I'd illuminated an entire row of the meanest-looking dogs I'd ever seen. There were five doghouses in a row against the back wall of the factory, and every pair of glowing eyes and gaping fangs were aimed at me. The rustling sounds were replaced with a low, rumbling growl that sounded like the roll of thunder.

Panic slowly creeping over me, I stayed completely still, fearing any move might send them lunging at me. I realized that my light was in my right hand and I couldn't even reach my nightstick or my gun without startling them into action. Even if I could get to my gun, how many of them could I shoot before the others got to me? My only option, I thought, was to keep the light steady on their eyes and very cautiously, very slowly, move towards the alleyway behind me. I was counting on getting a lot of space between us before I could break out into a cold sweat and a dead run.

Slowly, I moved my now-rubbery legs. With each movement I could hear the thunder growing. I could see the dogs slowly get up as if in unison. I took only two steps, and the nearest dog took his first lunge towards me. I started to run and felt the dog's jaws snapping at my heels. I looked over my shoulder and much to my relief I saw that this huge dog was chained. All I had to do was outrun the length of chain. I felt my fear subside slightly. But what a long chain it was! Finally, I could see it get taut and snap out straight. I slowed my pace and then saw the worst horror of my brief police career — THE CHAIN SNAPPED!

I'd experienced sheer terror, then relief, then absolute horror. My legs started moving so fast I'm sure only a blur could be seen. The huge animal continued to come at me like a furry cannonball. I then saw the police car near the end of the alleyway, and for a second I felt salvation was on the way. I quickly realized how close the animal was to my back and knew I had no time to go to the door of the police car. I took two more great strides and leapt onto the hood of the car, over the windshield, and wrapped my arms around the red roof-light. The light suddenly went on and there was no sound to be heard — except the hysterical laughter of my partner.

I looked over the edge of the roof of the car and saw him patting and scratching the ear of the huge beast, who had a few more woofs left in him. He had his paws up on the driver's door and, with his tongue hanging out and his tail wagging, looked up at me as if to say, "Thanks for the fun." My terrifying attack dog was suddenly an elderly, overweight, lovable mutt with no teeth. My partner knew the owner of the factory and also knew his beloved dogs were kept well fed and chained to their doghouses at the rear of the factory to keep prowlers away.

"Well," said my partner, "they sure do train you rookies better than when I was at the college. Why, I've never seen a rookie run as fast as *you* did!"

• • •

Hughie Brown, former Scotland Yard sergeant and a great raconteur, recalls a "baptism" he received at the very beginning of his career:

The Metropolitan Police Training School at Hendon in north London does an excellent job of preparing young officers for the streets, and for the thirteen weeks I was there I tried to cram as much as I could into my noggin. But they can't teach you everything. Some things you have to figure out — or learn the hard way.

"What's your name, young feller?" said the sergeant at Albany Street police station, the one I'd just been posted to.

"Brown," I replied.

"Well, young man, go with the van driver and pick up a drunk, will you?"

"Yes, Sergeant," I answered with zest.

I sought out the driver and we exchanged names. He told me that the longer a bloke's in the job the harder and more experienced he becomes. Boy, this guy's real experienced, I said to myself. Nice fellow, too.

We drove off in the van to locate this apparently unconscious female drunk — one of the local winos, the driver was told —

and bring her in to the station. We found her, as expected, and I was about to learn a thing or two about corralling a drunk.

"Open the back doors," said the van driver. "I'll grab her arms and you grab her legs and we'll lift her in, okay?"

"Right-o," I said, and grabbed the woman's ankles. We began to lift her into the van when she showered me with a well-aimed stream of urine.

The driver was in hysterics and said, "Lesson number one, young man, is always grab an arm and a leg and to hell with dignity!"

• • •

Oakville, Ontario, policeman Chris Perkins, who was a member of the illustrious Metropolitan Police (aka the Met and Scotland Yard) before immigrating to Canada, sent me a heap of hilarious tales from his years with the Met.

"The sheer size of the Met always seems to amaze my colleagues here," Chris told me. "Having two hundred police stations and 27,000 members makes for one hell of a large organization!"

One hell of a lot of horsing around, too, if Chris's tales are anything to go by. The police shenanigans in and around London, usually when most residents are sound asleep, are legion. Here's one example:

Every new probationer knows that sooner or later he or she will be expected to do something the rest of the shift has set up as a prank. Being wet behind the ears, I never knew when it might come. My particular initiation came by way of the telex, giving it an air of authenticity. I was given a copy of the telex printout. It was for an officer to take water samples.

Back then, impaired-driving suspects had the option of giving blood or urine samples. The divisional surgeon — a local on-call GP — was summoned to the station every time an impaired suspect came in. Every booking room had a small office attached called the divisional surgeon's room, and it stored needles, first-aid materials, and glass urine-sample bottles.

I was told to take several of these bottles, walk up to the canal that traversed our grounds, and take water samples every fifty paces, due to a complaint about water pollution. There I was, proud as punch and looking splendid in full uniform, on my knees scooping up samples of canal water.

My colleagues thought this was great fun and figured that, since I was such a good sport, why not continue the charade? They got a sergeant to visit me, and he explained that another telex had come through stating that, in addition to receiving water samples, the brass wanted to know the general flow, direction, and speed of the canal. I was given very explicit instructions to throw a leaf into the canal at a certain point; I was to time how long it took to float to another specific point, all the while making careful notes of my observations in my notebook. How they howled when I got back to the station for grub! I don't remember it being quite as funny as it seems now.

• • •

In his rookie year, policeman Michael L. Grant, of St. Johnsbury, Vermont, was involved in a case that really bugged him — in more ways than one. For weeks he and other officers had been trying in vain to capture a fleet-footed Peeping Tom who majored in motels. And then, one balmy July night, a tipster told Michael that the elusive voyeur was lurking around a certain motel. The young cop jumped into his car and drove to the brightly lit rear parking area of the building. And in Michael's own words this is what happened next:

I saw the man leaning against the building on one hand and looking in a bathroom window. He had one foot resting on a stone next to the building and was quite comfortable and content to watch what was going on inside.

The motel was about two hundred metres long in the back with no place for me to hide while sneaking up on him. He was about forty metres away. I knew the sergeant on duty that night was on his way. I stepped out slowly and started walking straight towards the peeper. I was ready to take off after him, if I had to, as soon as he spotted me. I had turned my portable radio down and didn't report what I was doing, because I didn't want the noise to scare him off. He didn't see me until I got about twenty metres from him.

He turned and saw me, and a look of guilt and fear came over him. In a split second he bolted. I yelled for him to stop, but he was in a dead run. So was I, and I pulled my radio out to tell the sergeant we'd be coming around the other side of the building.

Just as I opened my mouth a big bug flew in — right to the back of my throat. I had no choice but to try to swallow it while trying to talk over the radio. I managed to state that we'd be coming around the side and put my radio away while still running and choking on the stupid bug. I had chased this guy before, but this time he wasn't getting away, no matter what.

The far side of the motel was full of small gullies, rocks, and bushes. I guess because I was more of a country boy than he was I went straight through it, but it slowed him up considerably. When he saw that I was on him, he turned to give himself up. A few seconds later he was cuffed.

The worst — and most embarrassing — part was yet to come. The sergeant was just coming down the other side as I was escorting my prisoner up to his cruiser. We put him in the back seat, and the sergeant took me aside and asked, "Okay, now that you have him, what are you going to charge him with?"

In Vermont there's no law to prohibit people from looking in other people's windows. Being a new officer, I didn't know that, and of course I wasn't very happy about it.

I told the sergeant about the chase and the bug I almost choked on. When he stopped laughing he told me to give the guy a warning and let him go. The only thing I could think of to say was, "Sarge, that's a hard one to swallow."

• • •

A retired Scotland Yard bigwig, who wishes to remain anonymous, wrote to me about an unforgettable incident he investigated in days of yore:

In July 1955 I was a constable on night duty in Park Lane near Hyde Park, London. It was approximately 5:00 a.m. on a bright sunny morning. A car driving north towards Hyde Park Corner suddenly stopped, and a woman fully dressed in a long fur coat fell out or was pushed out. She was pretty intoxicated and was shouting abuse at the driver as he drove off in a hurry.

I was very new to my profession and had been on the beat only four months. I approached the woman, who was still making a great deal of noise, and as I got closer she took hold of the iron railing that surrounded the park. It was my intention to arrest her for drunkenness. In spite of much persuasion by me, and even threats, she would not let go of the railing. I therefore took hold of her in the region of her shoulders and pulled. There was a short struggle and I suddenly found the fur coat was off and there, clinging to the railing, was a completely naked woman, yelling and attracting the attention of early-morning motorists who were stopping to have a look. She was a prostitute, discarded by her client, but I was so green I did not cotton on, so to speak.

The audience of motorists was growing larger, and the comments they made were basically unprintable. I had a huge problem to solve: What part of the body of a naked woman, clinging to a railing in broad daylight, with a captive audience, does one take hold of to effect an arrest? The police-manual instruction of hammerlock (arm up the back) did not apply. Also, the manual did not give instructions on how to arrest naked women clinging to iron bars! Being too inexperienced to cope with such a problem, I really was upstream without a paddle.

After what seemed a lifetime, a more experienced constable appeared and he assessed the situation. I told him that the woman wouldn't let go of the railing. His reply was, "No problem," whereupon he took a lighter out of his pocket and ignited it. He gently caressed our naked lady with the flame on her posterior and she immediately leapt into the Black Maria and was taken to the station. In court she pleaded guilty to a charge of being drunk and disorderly and paid a fine. But the court never got to hear what really happened at that old iron fence.

• • •

Our good friend Detective Terry L. Davis, of Lemoore, California, sends this dandy reminiscence:

A field training officer — namely, me — was driving all over town, doing the night shift with a trainee. After a silent interval the trainer looked over at the trainee and saw that the sucker was asleep!

First of all, no police officer should allow himself to fall asleep on duty. If anybody had the right to fall asleep it was the seasoned officer, not the rookie. So, to teach this youngster a lesson, he used the thick fog over the city that night as an effective instructional tool.

He turned on the overhead reds and blues, slammed the car into park, jolting the trainee into a semiconscious state. He then yelled at the rookie, "CALL IT IN!" and, with that, immediately ran into an adjacent park and disappeared into the fog.

The rookie was totally lost. Call in *what?* So he did what he thought best — he ran after his partner, or at least where he *last saw* his partner.

The partner, in the meantime, circled around and got back in the car and drove off. It was about fifteen minutes before the trainee realized he'd been taught a lesson. But you can bet he never forgot it.

• • •

Chris Boyer of Kitchener, Ontario, recalls his first arrest as a student constable with the RCMP in Thompson, Manitoba:

One humid, mosquito-filled night in spring my partner and I received a call about a vandal stealing fire extinguishers from apartment complexes.

Upon arrival we spotted the culprit holding an extinguisher. He promptly dropped it and escaped into the dense northern Manitoba bush. We gave chase, but my partner advised me to stay put and wait for the police dog to pick up the trail.

As I hunkered down and turned up my collar to stave off the relentless mosquito attack, I soon could hear the unmistakable sound of someone nearby slapping mosquitoes. Clicking on my flashlight, I could see that it was none other than our suspect, less than fifteen feet away, being attacked by the merciless insects.

And that was how a mob of mosquitoes helped the Mounties get their man!

• • •

Because they're so wet behind the ears, rookie cops are often flabbergasted by offbeat and humorous things they see and/or hear while on duty. And in later years some of these now-seasoned coppers trot out their fondest and funniest memories and preserve them for a grateful posterity.

Earlier in this chapter former Scotland Yard officer Chris Perkins shared a rookie reminiscence. Now his father, Denis Perkins, offers to do the same. He writes:

Early August, 1959, at Blackheath Road police station — my first night out learning beats after graduating from the training school. They posted me with an old veteran of about twenty-five years. After parading at 10:00 p.m., we set off to our posted beat. I received the usual "Keep yer mouth shut and yer ears open" speech that every probationer has heard at one time or another. (I remember another useful item he taught me — "Remember, son, an hour off yer feet is worth a year on yer pension.") We arrived at Deptford High Street, the main thoroughfare of our beat, at about 10:30 p.m., and as we rounded a corner near a pub a strange thing happened.

Many pubs are situated on street corners, and still to this day many of them use a trap door in the sidewalk to accept delivery of barrels of ale. The trap doors open to reveal a metal ramp that's used to roll the barrels into the cellar of the pub. When the old sweat stepped onto the trap door, he stopped and thumped his foot twice. As he stepped off the wooden doors, one side opened up and a hand appeared holding a full pint glass of beer. My "parent police constable" reached down, grabbed the glass, and guzzled it in one swallow.

Without a word spoken, he put the glass on the windowsill of the pub and we carried on walking as if nothing had happened. He never mentioned it, and in my position as the new "sprog" I didn't have the nerve to ask him about it. What strikes me as odd to this day is the fact that nobody knew what beat they'd be on until they were paraded!

• • •

Annette McLoughlin of Dublin, Ireland, who describes herself as "forty-five going on eighteen," dropped a friendly line recently: One night, a young lady's twenty-first birthday party was held in our favourite local pub. We had ordered a Kiss-a-Gram for her, and as the hour was late we were getting anxious for the deliverer of this greeting to make his appearance. It's also the custom here in Ireland for the local police to drop in to the pubs if it's getting past closing time.

Anyway, next thing we knew, this very young policeman came into the pub. It was his first week on the beat, but we didn't know that yet, and everyone took him to be the Kiss-a-Gram fellow dressed up as a cop. So we all started shouting, "Okay, take them off, take them off!" The poor guy was nearly stripped while saying over and over, "I'll have to take your names." And, of course, we still thought it was a joke.

Minutes later, the man's sergeant came in and we all knew him. He confirmed that the partially clad copper was a new recruit. The poor young policeman ran out of the pub, as red-faced as could be.

• • •

Retired executive Russell D. Wallace of Halifax, Nova Scotia, had a brief career as a cop, serving with the RCMP in New Glasgow, Nova Scotia, between 1943 and 1946. Here's his account of a wacky case he was involved in back in his rookie year:

I was involved mostly with liquor work, which consisted mainly of raiding bootleggers, blacklisting suspected bootleggers, and searching for stills where illicit liquor was suspected of being made. I recall how another constable and I repeatedly raided a bungalow of a little old lady who was known to be a bootlegger. Search after search did not turn up any liquor on her premises — at least not until one day I took a different constable to raid with me and he had a stronger stomach than I did.

My fellow sleuth, himself a rookie, entered the old girl's bedroom and, as usual, just under the bed, was a chamber mug "floating full." He moved the malodorous item from under the bed, removed two loose floorboards, and there was the cache that put an end to the old girl's bootlegging days. The bungalow is long gone, and on the property there now stands an open-air theatre. I pass it frequently and it always makes me chuckle as I think of "the day the pot was moved."

7

Out of the Mouths of Babes

*Out of the mouths of babes and sucklings
hast thou ordained strength.*
— Psalms 8:2

As television performer Art Linkletter said, upwards of nine
million times, "Kids say the darnedest things."

They certainly do. And you can be sure they'll continue to do
so.

In my *Court Jesters* books we met a number of uncompli-
cated and undevious little folks who kept firing off truthful,
devastating, funny answers to questions tossed at them in the
witness box. Now we're going to look in on some other small-
fry and see how they fare in the world of cops.

The October 1954 issue of the RCMP *Quarterly* published a copy of an applicant's letter, neatly typed and received at the Lethbridge, Alberta, detachment of the world-famous force. It said:

> I am interested in receiving information concerning qualifications of entry into RCMP training. Could you advise me where to write, or could you supply this list of entry requirements for me?
>
> Also, where is the nearest RCMP training centre located?
>
> Thank you, in advance,
>
> Yours respectfully,
>
> Mr. Lee Nelson

The editor added this note: "We regret to advise that this applicant was turned down — Lee Nelson was found to be eight years of age."

• • •

A 1949 issue of the same publication reported the plight of a pair of young Ottawa boys who'd lost their dog. Their father heard them discussing possible ways of recovering their beloved pet and preserved this dialogue for posterity:

"Let's pray," suggested Bobby. "Maybe God will help."

"Shucks, no," replied Tom. "Let's tell the Mounties. They always get their man, and I bet they find missing dogs, too."

• • •

Dale Obermeyer, of Ancaster, Ontario, tells this story about one of her children and another well-known Canadian institution:

One summer evening I took my two sons to the local variety store to spend some of their allowance. As we approached the counter, Nicholas, my precocious five-year-old, noticed a police officer paying for a packet of gum.

Nicholas marched right up to the officer and, looking way up at him, blurted out, "What are you doing here? You're supposed to be at the Tim Horton's doughnut shop."

• • •

Betty Whiddington, of New York City, grew up in Owen Sound, Ontario, where her father, Charles C. Midddlebro', was for many years Crown Attorney for Grey County. She relates one of her dad's favourite tales:

The police in Owen Sound fell about laughing in 1958 when they heard that they were being asked to provide a certificate stating that Charles Richard Widddington, aged six months, had no criminal record in the County of Grey. This was a requirement for a visa to enter Argentina, where my husband and I and said child were going to live.

If they had known the little fellow two years later they might not have been so ready to give it!

• • •

Constable Shelley Ballard of Saskatoon, Saskatchewan, only one of thirteen female officers in a department of 360, often hears remarks pertaining to her gender. One in particular has always stood out in her memory:

I was working at the front desk of the police station one day when a gentleman came in to report a traffic accident. With the man was his young son, about four years old. The boy appeared very shy, and I tried to put him at ease by smiling and speaking to him. This really didn't work, however, and he continued to stare at me quite intently.

After I finished the report and he and his father were leaving the station, I heard the boy whisper in astonishment, "Daddy, that police*man* is a *girl!*"

• • •

Hey, Mum and Dad, what, pray tell, is going on after hours?

The December 1994 issue of an English police publication, *The Voice of the Service*, contains this informative little item supplied by an informative little bloke:

Sgt. Richard Wooley of Cheshire Police at Wilmslow was giving a talk to a class of seven-year-olds. He showed them a police truncheon, whereupon one little lad proudly announced: "My mummy's got one of those under her bed."

• • •

Jack While of Winnipeg, Manitoba, has many vivid memories of when he was a rookie policeman in the suburb of St. Vital, forty-plus years ago. Here's one of his favourite recollections from the comparatively innocent days of the early 1950s:

The best thing about being a police officer, particularly if you grew up in the community in which you serve, is the fact that you know ninety percent of the residents and, for the most part, grew up knowing the men who've become your senior officers.

My deputy chief constable was a big-boned, hard-nosed World War I sergeant-major I'd known for years. When I enlisted in the police department, he was on in years and spent most of his time as an administrator. He pretty well came and went as he saw fit but was still the tough, grisly oldster he'd been thirty years before. He would come in on a Sunday after church to prepare the following week's duty roster, court dockets, etc. He had mountains of experience, and though he'd mellowed a great deal, he was still a man to be reckoned with.

One Sunday I was patrolling in a cruiser and received a radio message that a fourteen-year-old girl had not come home from a school dance. I knew her, as well as her friends. Preliminary inquiries were made of the school staff, chaperons, and families of her friends, but nothing constructive was learned.

I continued on patrol and observed the car of a youth known to keep company with the missing girl. I approached his vehicle, pulled him over, and found the girl asleep, slouched over in the front seat. The young man was directed to follow me in his car to the police office. The young lady travelled with me in the cruiser.

At the station the deputy chief spoke to the girl while I questioned the young man. He seemed straightforward and claimed that they'd left the dance and gone for a drive when the car became stuck on a little-used mud road. He said it had taken hours to arrange help to get the car free, and he added that he was taking the girl home when I stopped him.

Meanwhile, the deputy chief had interviewed the girl, and she, too, said that nothing untoward had occurred except that she was late getting home. He left her sitting in the office and joined me. He asked me what I had learned, indicating he was about to notify the girl's parents and he wanted to be sure everything was in order. I told him the young man's story and his reason for being so late.

The deputy chief returned to the girl and told her in a most uncharacteristic and fatherly voice that she'd caused a lot of worry for her parents and the school staff.

He then asked, "Where did you get stuck?" She hesitated, looked down at the floor and replied, "In the back seat."

• • •

A veteran of the now-defunct British Columbia Provincial Police recalls that while on a long patrol in the 1930s he was given overnight lodgings by a couple who owned a small ranch in the province's Cariboo region:

After we had enjoyed a fine dinner, my hosts broke the news

that I would have to sleep with their small son as they didn't have a spare bed. The privy was outdoors, so a lard pail or some such container was left under the bed for emergencies. Some folks called that sort of receptacle the "goesunder."

The little fellow and I got undressed and ready for bed. He knelt down on the floor, resting his elbows on the bed. I thought he was saying his prayers and decided to follow his example or the kid might think badly of me. Down I got, put my hands together, and tried to remember the Lord's Prayer.

Suddenly the lad called out, "Hey, mister, what are you doing?"

"Same as you, son," I said.

"Gee, mister," he replied, "Mom will give you heck in the morning. There's no pot on your side."

• • •

It's amazing — and sometimes amusing — how certain child-hood memories keep returning. They're often triggered by a sight, a sound, a smell, or some other stimulus, but sometimes they pop into the mind for no apparent reason. That's the way it's been with Alex McKay, who's lived all his life in the small town of Portsoy, Scotland.

Alex was just a wee lad when he had his first brush with the law, and whenever he recalls the event he immediately starts to chuckle.

"Just before the start of World War II, when I was only about six, I started chopping down a tall pole near our home," he says. "I kept hacking away with a small hatchet and the pole started to sway. Just then I heard someone coming around the corner on a bicycle. I dropped the hatchet and put my hand on the pole to stop it from falling. Then, lo and behold, the local bobby rode up on his bike."

The bobby asked Alex, "What are you doing here at this time of night? It's nearly seven o'clock."

Alex said he was holding up the pole, and the bobby told him not to be cheeky and get along home. But Alex didn't budge.

"I still stood there," he reports, "so the policeman took hold of my arm and pulled me away from the pole, which immediately started to fall. He looked up, flabbergasted and frightened, and I shouted, '*I told you so*,' and ran like hell."

Two minutes later the bobby was at Alex's front door, returning the hatchet to his mother. He said to Alex in a kindly way, "Learning to be a lumberjack, are you? Don't worry, laddie, it was an old pole that was due to come down soon anyway. There's no harm done, my boy."

Alex recalls that his mother bawled him out, but his father had a good laugh when he heard about the incident.

"I've never forgotten the look on that bobby's face when I let go of the pole and it started to fall," says Alex. "And I'm sure I never will."

• • •

Back in the 1960s a police officer in another small town — Fergus, Ontario — blew the whistle on a pint-sized accomplice.

"In those days there were no parking meters in the town," the officer recalls, "so policemen would put a chalk mark on one of the tires of cars that had been parked for the limit of two hours. About two and a half hours after a certain car had been parked, I was about to issue a ticket when a boy of about ten asked me if I was issuing a ticket for his father's vehicle, and I said yes.

The little lad frowned and said to the officer, "Uh-oh, I'm in trouble now because I was supposed to wipe off the chalk mark."

• • •

Constable Jack MacNeill, of the Charlottetown, Prince Edward Island detachment of the Royal Canadian Mounted Police, will never forget Christmas of 1992. Jack tells this touching tale:

In the wee hours of Christmas morning, I was roused from my

bed to respond to a burglar alarm at a local business. I was up, dressed, and out the door without realizing I'd left my portable radio at my bedside. While en route to the scene, the police car hit a patch of ice and spun me into a deep snowbank. I sheepishly radioed our dispatcher to summon a towtruck to rescue me from my predicament.

When the dispatcher asked what happened, I thought I'd make light of the situation by telling her I'd swerved to avoid what looked to be a sleigh drawn by eight reindeer on the road ahead.

About an hour later, I returned home and was met by my wife and seven-year-old daughter who, unbeknownst to me, had jumped into bed beside her mother and had monitored my transmissions on the police radio I'd left behind.

I'll never forget the look of awe and wonder in my daughter's eyes when she hugged me and exclaimed, "Daddy, you saved Santa!"

8

The Mounties

I never did like that emblim they have up on the wall —
"We always gits our man." Fur a change, they deserves to
git the gurl. It's helthier.
— Don Harron
(alias Charlie Farquharson)

It's hard to believe that the Mounties have been battling crime in
the world's second-largest country since away back in 1873 —
originally as the North-West Mounted Police, then as the Royal
North-West Mounted Police, and finally, in 1920, as the Royal
Canadian Mounted Police.

The RCMP has grown from 300 to 16,000 members, and for
the past sixty years or so, thanks largely to Hollywood, the force
has been admired greatly around the globe. That situation

inspired internationally acclaimed Canadian author Margaret Atwood to note: "Canada must be the only country in the world where a policeman is used as a national symbol; the Canadian contestant in Miss Universe contests invariably wears a cute Mountie uniform."

So let's take a lighthearted look at the Mounties, eh?

The late Mr. Justice Stuart Purvis, of the Court of Queen's Bench of Alberta, wrote to me about prairie justice in earlier and simpler times:

When I was a teenager in the village of Viking, ninety miles east of Edmonton, Chief Judge Lucien Dubuc of the Alberta District Court presided over court on a regular basis in the village library. The sessions proved to be popular entertainment, and the characters involved always played to a full house.

On one occasion, in the late 1930s, my father, a lawyer, was defending an alleged horse thief. About halfway through the proceedings, Chief Judge Dubuc inquired, "Mr. Purvis, where is your client?"

Much to the mortification of defence counsel and six-foot-four Corporal "Tiny" Bain of the Royal Canadian Mounted Police, the accused had disappeared!

After a frantic search, the police surrounded the outhouse at the back of the library building and apprehended the miscreant as he emerged after having unobtrusively and innocently answered a call of nature.

The Mounties always get their man!

• • •

In answer to the question, "Why do you wish to join the Royal Canadian Mounted Police?" one confident young man wrote, "Because I look good in a uniform and would be a joy to behold."

Another applicant, answering the same question, stated with irrefutable logic: "By living like a man when I am young I will add years to my life when I become old."

And a third chap said he had an excellent reason for wanting to join the RCMP: "I am not fussy on getting married, but I can't help but fall for every girl I meet, and since you will not give permission until after five years of service, I feel quite sure I will know better by then."

• • •

Every active or retired Mountie has his or her own registration number, which for official purposes is practically part of his or her name — for example, "Reg. No. 26540, John Smith."

Back in 1952, the Halifax *Chronicle-Herald* reported this alleged snippet of dialogue between a local man and his lovestruck daughter:

DAD: It seems to me, Mary, that you wish to rush into marriage very hastily. What is the policeman's name?

MARY: I don't know his name, Dad, but I've sure got his number.

• • •

"Things are looking up in our recruiting campaign," wrote the editor of the RCMP *Quarterly* in 1954 — twenty years before the force opened its ranks to women. He offered as proof this epistle from six ardent applicants whose names he altered:

Nurses' Residence
St. Joseph's Hospital

Dear RCMP:

We noticed in the *Pembroke Bulletin* last week an urgent plea for recruits for the RCMP. It did not specify whether male or female recruits were desired, therefore we are taking this opportunity of writing for further information. We also carry the motto of the RCMP, i.e., "We Are Out to Get Our Men."

As for qualifications, we have almost completed our "probie" term in nursing. Nearly all are 5'8", single (darn it!), completed our 4th form in high school, all average 19 years of age, chest expansion 37" more or less.

Height — **A.** Blank — 5'8" in bare feet
        B. Black — 5'7" in Cuban heels
        C. White — 5'8" in 6" spikes
        D. Green — 5'6" in 2" platform shoes
        E. Grey — 5'7" in Oxfords
        F. Brown — 5'5" — but eager

Thanking you for your invitation, and eagerly awaiting your reply,

Yours hopefully,
Future RCMPs
per (sgd.)

• • •

No doubt inspired by the Nelson Eddy and Jeanette MacDonald movie, *Rose Marie*, which was all the rage in 1936, a man purportedly applying for employment with the RCMP scribbled out this lively letter and fired it off to national headquarters:

Dear Sir and Major:

I have read in the newspapers that you are looking for recruits.

I beg Sir and Major to give you the chance of getting my services as I want to enlist. My qualifications follow.

I have the real detective instink. Also my brother-in-law tells me I would make good as a Mountie in moving picture work, which I understand is all you do now in Canada, outside of detective work. I can ride well — although I understand from friends of mine who saw your troops that the horses follow each other round and round, so good riding is not an essential.

I also understand dogs, having bred pomeranians, as I understand you use dogs in some of your winter pictures. Socially I am well informed, I can dance — can act like a gentleman if you should need me in a character part. I understand when you get assignments like you are on in New York now you have to behave properly, so in this I am quite at home. I rarely drink, but can if it is necessary for some picture or another.

If it is all the same to you I would like to start at a little better than a private, a corporal for example, although personally I would like to be a Sgt. Major, as I understand he does not clean his horse — and I forgot to say I am not over strong, although I know I can do all you have to do in summer Mountie pictures. The winter ones might be a little strenuous at the start.

I am 27 — married — although my wife says if I go into the movies to hell with you, so you see I am nearly single — for I understand you only take <u>officially</u> single men.

As for location I will go anywhere only I don't like too much snow. I have friends near Medicine Hat, so I shall be near them if you could arrange for me to go to Ottawa.

So Sir and Major I ask that you reply at once to me as my business is almost finished for the time being — that is I know the Mountie business will pay me more than a restaurant, as I feel sure they must pay you real money for pictures, endorsing cigarettes etc.

Please reply where I can go to get medical examination to join, although I don't need it as I am A.1. perfect — 6'0", 185 lbs., slightly flat feet although you would never suspect it, but in riding it would not show. I will drive in at once if you will send a telegram collect, as money is no object if I can get a good position with you as Sgt. Major — or less.

Respectfully, dear Sir and Major.

• • •

Ain't love grand? The RCMP *Quarterly* of April 1951 carried this heart-tugging tale:

Cupid in Court

On March 28, 1950, a resident of the Lestock District of Saskatchewan was charged with carnal knowledge of a girl under fourteen years of age, the girl having previously given birth to a baby daughter. When the accused was arraigned in court before a police magistrate, it was pointed out that he was anxious to marry the girl in question. The magistrate stated that if there was any chance of the couple getting married, he would adjourn the case and consider suspended sentence.

On April 1 the accused was again brought before the court with members of the Social Welfare Department present, as well as two members of the RCMP. In the meantime the couple had got together and decided to get married. However, it was found that although all other preparations had been looked after, nothing had been done with regard to witnesses, and as the man involved was still in custody, two members of the RCMP were called upon to serve as witnesses to the wedding, as well as act as the prisoner's guard.

The wedding took place in the United Church manse at

Melville, and during the ceremony it was revealed that the husband-to-be did not have a ring. To avoid further delay, one of the policemen handed him his RCMP-crested ring, which — although almost large enough to be a bracelet for the bride — served the purpose. During the ceremony, the Social Welfare officer acted as "baby-sitter" and when it came time to sign the register one Mounted Policeman attending signed in the space allotted for the best man, while the other signed as bridesmaid.

After the service the prisoner was taken before the court and the magistrate saw fit to impose suspended sentence with his blessing.

• • •

Many events that are terribly serious when they transpire become funny later, when the heat's off, so to speak.

Sergeant Brian Rogers, in his quarter-century with the RCMP, has experienced this hundreds of times, as have countless cops the world over. Brian serves with the RCMP in Regina, Saskatchewan, and he has never been accused of being dull or solemn. According to his wife, Sheila, he's completely down-to-earth and disgustingly cheerful — all the time.

"Brian has a great sense of humour," she says. "He sees the bright side of everything. He's always optimistic. In 1994, when he served with the United Nations peacekeeping force in Bosnia, everyone at the Regina detachment looked forward to his return because they missed his laughter and joking around."

Over the course of his career Sergeant Brian Rogers has had a great many adventures, and no matter how godawful the circumstances, his sense of humour never deserted him. Two hair-raising fiascoes he was involved in are presented herewith, narrated by Brian himself. Here's the first:

The Photo Op from Hell

The Mounties hold quite an honourable position in a lot of the prairie communities in Canada. We usually are asked to participate in a number of parades during our service. Such was the case for me during the summer of 1977. The town of Drumheller, Alberta, was holding a Dominion Day parade and requested that a member of the RCMP lead it. Since I'd just recently transferred to Drumheller from the Musical Ride in Ottawa, I was advised by my sergeant that I would have this honour. He said I could either march or ride a horse. Since I'm much more comfortable in a saddle, I selected the latter.

I had made arrangements with a local doctor to use his horse. Pokey was a quarter horse and ex-pickup horse from the rodeo circuit. The doctor advised me that Pokey was extremely good in crowds and would be no problem in the parade. What I did not know until the day of the parade was that he had not been ridden in five years.

The ranch where Pokey was living the life of Riley was five miles from Drumheller, so on the night before the parade I went to the ranch to bring him into Drumheller. Since the doctor did not have a horse trailer, I opted to ride him the five miles into town. I felt this would be a good opportunity to get a feel for Pokey. The whole five miles was a rodeo, with Pokey bucking all the way. I managed to stay with him and avoid hitting the dirt. I kept him that night at another Mountie's acreage and hoped I had worn the edge off him.

The next morning I rose early so I could give Pokey a good grooming and polish the RCMP tack I would use on him. With the RCMP ceremonial tack, Pokey was a sight to behold. He was a very proud-looking animal and carried himself with honour. I dressed in my typical RCMP red serge coat and mounted him.

The parade was to start in front of the Drumheller hospital at 9:00 a.m. sharp. Of course, the proud doctor was there to take some pictures, which I assumed would hold a position of great honour in his office. Pokey was a little more manageable than he had been the previous night. I assumed my fine equestrian skills had let him know who was the boss.

I took my place at the front of the parade and moments later was joined by the Drumheller Legion Band, who were armed with plenty of bagpipes. I don't think Pokey had any Scottish blood, because he sure didn't like the sound of the bagpipes. He immediately broke into a sweat and tried to rear up and buck. The local fire department, whose members I knew quite well, were taking bets on when I would hit the pavement. My pride wouldn't allow that to happen. The good doctor came over and requested that I bring Pokey over to the lawn in front of the hospital for a photo session. I would do anything to keep that horse moving and away from the band.

As I positioned Pokey on the lawn in front of the hospital, I felt his hindquarters drop. I thought he was going to rear up again, so I pulled on the reins to keep his head up. He dropped farther, and when I looked down I noticed he was sinking into a hole. I immediately jumped to the sidewalk as Pokey disappeared from view. The earth had swallowed my horse whole, including the tack I'd spent several hours polishing.

The hole that Pokey had fallen into was an abandoned septic-tank excavation from yesteryear. The opening was thirty inches by thirty inches and eight feet deep. It had been covered by wood after World War II and became weakened from rot.

Unfortunately the horse and I were in the wrong place at the wrong time. I spent several minutes staring down at this huge animal and wondering how I would ever get him out of there. I recall thinking that I might have to *march* in the parade, which is a disgrace for a member of the Mounted Police who wears the badge of the Musical Ride proudly on his red serge.

Suddenly, from the crowd, came the voice of a very intoxicated cowboy. "I'll save that horse!" he announced, then jumped into the hole, not knowing how deep it was or where it would lead. Soon I was relieved to hear him shout, "Get a vet!"

At that very moment, my sergeant came up to me and said, "Rogers, let's get this parade on the road!" I advised him that my horse was down in this hole and I could not go. He thought maybe I had finally cracked under the strain of police work in Drumheller. When he looked into the hole he saw the faces of two animals, one a horse that was sober and the other a cowboy who was drunk.

The veterinarian arrived within minutes and, with the help of a boom from the local telephone company, they lowered the doctor into the hole. The first item to emerge from the hole was the highly polished ceremonial tack, which was covered in mud and hacked to death by the drunken cowboy's jackknife. The vet gave Pokey some medicine to calm him down and asked for some rope to cinch the horse's front legs. Then they pulled Pokey from the hole by his front legs. The only injury he received was a small cut to his chest, possibly caused by the cowboy's knife.

It was far too late for me to participate in the parade, and Pokey was in no condition to go anywhere, except back to the ranch to sleep it off. I returned to my detachment and went on patrol that night in Drumheller.

While I was on foot patrol through the local bars I heard a familiar voice cry, "Howdy!" It was my friend the boozed-up cowboy, who was even more inebriated now. He was telling his friends the story of Pokey in the septic tank and they thought he was crazy. He was very glad to see me and very grateful that I came to his rescue, for I told his friends that his story was true. I asked him if he was going to be driving that night, and he laughed and said, "Nah, I'll just find some hole to fall into."

• • •

A few years later, Brian Rogers was transferred to the RCMP detachment in Whitehorse, Yukon, where he did mainly office work and served on the side as team leader for the Emergency Response Team — a SWAT-type outfit known as ERT for short. That's where he had his next excellent adventure.

We Weren't Jumping for Joy

In the summer of 1987, we received a call from our detachment at Beaver Creek, Yukon, a hamlet of sixty-five people, including one Mountie, smack on the border between Yukon and Alaska. One night the man working at the Beaver Creek airport informed the detachment that he saw two men cross the border on the airstrip. He reported that when he approached them they fired at his vehicle with a high-powered rifle. He said he returned fire and the men retreated to the heavy bush around the airport. Our informant also advised that when he returned to the airport terminal the men fired at him again.

The ERT was alerted around 2:00 a.m. and a dozen of us — Pilot Gerry Anderson, Commander Jim Cairns, P.J. Thompson, Dwight Berkner, Sandy Ervin, Rick Mosher, Harold Milroy, Eric Wheeler, Gary Williams, Ron Pond, Will Leduc, and myself — flew off to Beaver Creek on the RCMP Twin Otter plane.

The flight to Beaver Creek takes about an hour and a half, and I knew we'd be landing in daylight. Since the culprits were supposed to be in the bush somewhere along the airstrip, I'd come up with a plan that would allow us to land the plane and unload our equipment in safety. The airstrip is gravel and lined with bush. I decided to have the pilot do a short landing, immediately turn the plane, stop, and then I'd leave the plane by the rear emergency exit, along with three other assault members. We'd then take up positions along the strip to give cover for the rest of the team. All this planning took place at the back of the plane, and I assumed that the information would be relayed to the pilot. I assumed wrongly.

We approached Beaver Creek at approximately 4:00 a.m., and the assault members were braced at the rear emergency exit. The plane touched down and immediately started to brake. When the plane made its turn I opened the door and jumped with my M-16 in my hand. The distance from the tail of the plane to the ground was about seven feet. I could hear the roar of the engine, but I couldn't see the ground for dust. I thought the pilot was back-feathering his engines to brake, but he was actually giving it full throttle to go towards the terminal.

When my feet hit the ground it was like landing on a conveyor belt. I was the first man out of the plane, so the speed was only around ten miles an hour. By the time the final man left the plane, the speed had reached forty-five miles an hour. When I glanced back at the plane, it looked like unwanted luggage was coming out the rear door. Only the first two of us to hit the tarmac could do anything to guard the plane. The other two jumpers received minor cuts and bruises and lost their M-16s, and they had a hard time just trying to figure out where they were.

Apparently the pilot did not receive the full instructions and thought he would do a short landing and immediately go to the terminal where we would leave the plane from the rear exit and provide cover for the rest of the assault team. When he realized we were leaving the plane while it was still on the landing strip, he put on the brakes. But it was too late. We were already out.

I remained in the bush along with the other member who wasn't hurt. The other two had to find their guns and then crawl to the terminal to be bandaged. We remained in position for four hours, not hearing a sound. Finally the commander called us in and we did a search of the bush with the police dog. We found no trace of any would-be criminals. We then spoke with the man who'd called in the complaint, and after an hour of grilling he confessed that he made the story up just to get attention!

We all got together and had lunch, and before we left Beaver Creek, posed in front of the police plane to have our picture taken. Upon our return to Whitehorse, word soon got around the detachment that we had jumped out of our plane while it was still moving. Within minutes, some wag dubbed us the HURT assault team.

Our outfit's newsletter immediately shed the ERT part of its title and was renamed *The HURT Team Dispatch*. It also acquired a new motto, "We jump at Dawn . . . or Sally or Mary or . . ." and published this weather forecast for the Beaver Creek area: "Partly cloudy with scattered HURT members towards dawn."

An item in the *Dispatch* twitted one of the team members: "We have a confirmed report that Hollywood will be making a movie of the incident. The title of the film will be *Throw Milroy from the Plane*, starring Danny Devito as Harold Milroy." An accompanying cartoon showed a man swathed in bandages from head to toe being urged by a hospital visitor: "Hurry up and get better, Dwight. Brian wants us to go to Skagway next week and jump off a train."

• • •

In Prince Edward Island in August of 1994, a newsletter published by the Royal Canadian Mounted Police saluted "the Mountie of the Month," an officer who, in the words of the publication, "overcame adversity and lack of available backup (what else is new?) to triumph over the forces of evil."

The newsletter, describing the aftermath of a three-man jail-break, continued its colourful report:

"Like salmon going home to spawn, the trio made their way to their respective homes, one of which was located near Alberton, P.E.I. Acting on a tip, Constable Karen Traverse and another officer drove to the residence of one of the subjects, only to have him run for the woods. Constable Traverse, not having an intimate knowledge of this particular woodland, and not having sufficient backup to effectively cordon off the area, then improvised in a way that would put many veteran members to shame.

"The suspect's own dog was sufficiently disturbed by the racket of police arriving and owner departing that he started barking in the direction in which his master had fled. It was at this point that the imaginative policewoman, using the jargon of the region, hollered to the felon that a police dog was about to give chase and grievous bodily harm could result."

In the interest of historical accuracy, I must intervene and tell you what the officer *really* shouted to the fugitive, as revealed to me by an unimpeachable RCMP source. Fully aware that the only canine in the vicinity was owned by the fellow in the woods, the fearless Constable Traverse bellowed with all her might:

"WE HAVE A POLICE DOG HERE WHO'S GOING TO BITE YOUR ASS OFF UNLESS YOU SURRENDER IMMEDIATELY!"

"And," says my informant, "the bad guy came out with his arms high in the air, brought to justice by the barking of his own dog."

• • •

Corporal Andrew Black, of the RCMP in Ottawa, recently confessed in print that more than a decade ago he'd wantonly disregarded a sacred rule of his employer and, as a result, got his just desserts. In a short humorous report entitled "Headdress, and Why It Should Be Worn," Andy Black rats on himself:

"At Fork River, Manitoba, at 9:40 p.m., May 5, 1984, I stopped a Volkswagen bus with a defective headlight. On exiting the police car, I deliberately refrained from donning my headdress, in violation of an RCMP regulation to the contrary. While questioning the bus driver, I suddenly lost the sight in my right eye and felt cold moisture on my cheek. As foul weather had been forecast, I assumed it had begun to rain. However, no raindrops followed. I then thought that possibly the bus driver had spit in my face, but I realized I would have seen it coming.

"I removed my glasses and noticed that the right lens was covered with a dark substance. At the same time, a flock of gulls could be heard laughing overhead. I realized my problem and excused myself to clean up while my chuckling partner finished the spot check, headdress intact."

The now-penitent corporal says he's grateful he wasn't hauled up on the carpet for the hat violation.

"If I had," he notes succinctly, "I would have been crapped on twice." Corporal Black said he later remembered a poem he'd learned as a boy. A silly little verse with "a lot of relevance" to the events described above, it goes like this:

> Birdie, birdie, in the sky,
> Why'd you do that in my eye?
> I'll be brave and I won't cry,
> I'm just glad that cows don't fly!

• • •

Chief Judge Harold Gyles, of the Provincial Court of Manitoba, told me a story of great educational value to cops. He supplied me with a transcript of the testimony given by a man charged with obstructing a highway.

"The case was tried in the mid-1960s," His Honour advised, "and there's such a good lesson in here for overzealous policemen that most RCMP recruits who've come along since then have received a copy of this transcript for careful consideration."

After a Mountie had testified, the judge asked the accused, "Is there anything you wish to say?"

"There certainly is, sir," the man replied.

"All right," said the judge, "please take the witness box."

Word for word, here's the entire testimony of the accused:

I was on my way to buy hay for a horse ranch that I have down on No. 4 Highway. My ranch foreman was in a car proceeding north ahead of me. He didn't know this cutoff to go down to No. 59 on the Perimiter Highway. So I swung around the corner, going east, partway toward the underpass. I stopped my car — it was running — and I opened the door and was honking my horn and waving at him to come back.

Our farm is about ten miles past that, where we breed racehorses, and we were out to buy hay that afternoon. We were

175

going to Bird's Hill, and he went past and didn't know where to turn off, so I turned partially in there and was honking and waving my arms, and he stopped on the overpass when the officer came up behind me.

Now he came up behind me, and as an officer of the law I don't think he was justified in what he was doing, because first of all he says, "Pull up ahead, there," which I did, and he grabs a plastic jug out of my car. I am a responsible citizen. I don't use home brew. I have a farm and everything. He pulls the jug out of my car and pours some in his hand and licks at it like a dog [demonstrating], which is true as long as I stand here and hold this Bible.

What he was looking for, I don't know. He wanted to give me a ticket and he didn't know what to give it for, and that's all it was. And if he knew what I carried in that bottle, he wouldn't have licked the stuff out of that bottle, let me tell you.

I have breeding mares, and I take the urine to the vet all the time, and that's what I use the bottle for, and that is the honest-to-God truth. And he had to give me a ticket for something, because he figured he got to give me a ticket, that's all."

JUDGE: For tasting your sample?

ACCUSED: I guess it tasted so good he wanted to know where I lived, to get more.

JUDGE: Thank you very much. I am going to acquit you.

• • •

You met Constable Duncan Chisholm of the RCMP in chapters one and two. He's a quick-witted six-footer from Quebec, presently stationed at Deer Lake, Newfoundland. In seventeen memory-packed years as a Mountie he's also served in the Newfoundland communities of Labrador City, St. John's, Holyrood, and Bonavista, as well as in Fort McPherson and Inuvik in the Northwest Territories.

When it comes to telling humorous tales about the police work he loves dearly, Duncan's memory seldom lets him down.

But he sometimes needs a nudge — you might raise a new subject, for instance, or ask if he's ever had a certain kind of case — and then, to swipe a phrase from Marcel Proust, "suddenly the memory returns."

And how! When recollecting a funny story, Dunc Chisholm frequently reminds himself of two or three others, as well. He sees fun and humour nearly everywhere, but essentially he's a hardworking, serious cop.

And he's been that way from the beginning.

In the summer of 1978, after he'd survived six months of extremely rigorous training, the brand-new Mountie, Constable Duncan Chisholm, was sent to fill in for the regular officer at a detachment on the northeast coast of Labrador. About half an hour after arriving, decked out in jeans, T-shirt, and baseball cap, he took his fishing rod from the trunk of his car and walked out on the government wharf to see if he could catch himself an Arctic char.

A few minutes after he'd started fishing, he felt someone tap him on the shoulder. He turned around and a man said, "You pay me twenty bucks. You fish in my water. Me Chief."

Duncan had been introduced to the *real* chief twenty minutes earlier, and this was not the same guy.

"I introduced myself as the new constable," Chisholm says. "He took one look at me and lit out of there like his pants were on fire. I was in town for the next six weeks, and whenever he spotted me he ran away and hid. But I heard during my stay that quite a few tourists coughed up the twenty dollars."

• • •

Dunc recalls a fall evening in 1991, during moose-hunting season, when the Mounties got something other than their man:

RCMP Constable Dave Gosine was on routine patrol outside Bonavista, Newfoundland. It was just getting dark and he saw a light on the edge of a field. He parked his police cruiser and started to walk towards a couple of men in the woods.

The men hadn't seen him and he could hear them talking among themselves. As he crouched down in the bushes he clearly heard one man say to the other, "Hurry up, get the saw."

Well, Dave figured he'd discovered some moose poachers in action. He called out the troops on his portable radio, and Sergeant John Bishop and I rushed to Dave's aid. We arrived a few minutes later — just in time, it appeared, as a pickup truck was coming out the road that led from the woods. We had the poachers boxed in!

They stopped in the middle of the road, to our surprise. We asked them to show their moose licence and, lo and behold, in the back of the truck was a butchered *cow*! The men had carved up their own animal on their own property. Some poachers! No wonder they laughed when we started to question them.

The next day Dave got a lot of mooooos when he went for his morning pick-me-up at the local coffee shop. A group of citizens even composed and sang a song they called "The Mountie Got His Moose."

• • •

There was a time, a decade or so ago, when Duncan was considered — by some, at least — the Davy Crockett of the Far North. His shooting skill bagged him funny yarns to tell when he'd switched to shooting the breeze. Here's a sample:

One day in March 1985, I was on the Dempster Highway between Fort McPherson and Inuvik, in the Northwest Territories, transporting a prisoner in the back of the RCMP paddy wagon. It was minus forty Celsius and our jail guard asked me if I saw a rabbit along the way to please get it for his supper.

I was thirty miles outside town and saw this big rabbit about fifty yards from the edge of the bush. I got out of the vehicle, pulled my revolver, and fired at it. I couldn't believe my eyes. The rabbit did a somersault and dropped dead in his tracks. The snow was really light and I knew if I went after the rabbit I'd sink up to my neck.

I looked at the prisoner, who didn't weigh much, and said, "Get me that rabbit."

He took a good look at me and said, "Don't worry, I won't run away — not from a guy who can shoot like that!"

• • •

Police officers often have to be resourceful, and in the story that follows Constable Chisholm reveals just how resourceful he can be when he really puts his mind to it:

In 1988 in Inuvik, I was investigating a rash of minor house breaks and had a few suspects to check out. There were three fellows I heard were responsible. I drove around town and saw one of them walking down the street. I motioned for him to have a seat in the police car. He had a few drinks under his belt, and he wasn't the brightest chap I've ever met.

I questioned him for ten minutes and he wouldn't confess. I then asked him if he knew what a lie detector was, and he said no. On the seat beside me I had a screening device for motorists suspected of driving while impaired. It registers one of three different verdicts — "Pass," "Warning," or "Fail."

I told my suspect I was going to have him blow into the machine and it would tell us whether he was guilty or not. I said if he blew "Pass" it meant he knew nothing about the break-ins; if he blew "Warning" it indicated he wasn't guilty but knew who was; and if he blew "Fail" it meant he was one of the guys who broke into the houses.

To my delight, he blew "Fail." I looked at him and said, "Well?" He said, "You got me!" and confessed to a bunch of break-ins.

I tried it again on others, but no one else would bite.

• • •

The irrepressible Duncan Chisholm also displayed a lot of inge-
nuity in the investigation of another incident:

When I was stationed in Bonavista in 1992, I was on patrol in
Plate Cove and drove up to the government wharf. I saw two fellows at the end of the wharf, and when they saw me they threw
their beer in the ocean. I caught one guy as he came towards
me to get off the wharf, and I charged him with drinking in public. He wouldn't say who his buddy was and I didn't see him
leave the wharf.

I walked around the wharf and looked down into the boats as
I passed by. From about three metres above, I could see a bit of
this fellow's foot — he was hidden under some slabs of wood
over the fish-holding area in the boat. I walked back to the car
and waited for the fellow to come out, as he must have been getting a bit wet by now and, being in the fish bin, would be starting
to smell. But he stayed put.

I had a Coke bottle in the cruiser. I filled it full of water and
walked back to the edge of the wharf just above where the guy
was hiding. I wasn't sure if he could see me through the slats in
the wood covering the fish bin. It was very quiet at that time.

I said loudly, to no one in particular, "I gotta have a leak!"

I opened my zipper, which I was sure he could hear, and I
started pouring water from the Coke bottle onto the fish bin.
Well, you've never seen anyone scoot as fast as this guy did
when he left his hiding place! When he saw me with a big grin
on my face and a bottle in my hand, he knew he'd been had.

• • •

As we've seen, Constable Chisholm is rather unorthodox from
time to time. The way he handled a nuisance caller proves that
— in spades:

In 1988 in Labrador City, I arrested a fellow for impaired driving. After failing the Breathalyzer test he was released around 4:15 a.m. I drpve him home and returned to the detachment, where my duty was to monitor the telephones.

Well, it wasn't long before the phones started ringing and ringing and ringing, with this guy just breathing into the telephone. This went on for well over an hour. I would put all the lines on hold for a few minutes and then take them off. The phone would ring again, and as soon as I picked it up he'd be there breathing. It was now 6:00 a.m.

One of the more senior fellows told me how to take a bullet apart and fire the blank into the telephone. He said the noise on the other end would be ten times louder than on my end. The phone rang again. I picked up the receiver and made sure it was my breather calling. Then I fired a blank and put the receiver to my ear. I could hear him scream on the other end.

I drove to the local hospital and, sure enough, along he came, holding his ear. I pointed at him and said, "*Gotcha!*" I didn't get any more breathing calls after that.

• • •

Some folks are remembered for ages because of a funny line they once uttered. Retired Mountie Joseph T. Parsons wrote about such a person in an RCMP anthology of memories entitled *The Way It Was*:

In the early thirties, I was detailed along with many other young constables for Doukhobor patrols in Saskatchewan, as the Sons of Freedom sect had become very restless and had been setting the torch to schools and other public buildings. Constable Matt Medlyn, now deceased, was my sidekick.

The town of Kamsack, where we were billeted, had a mixture of many different nationalities. The feeling was quite anti-Doukhobor as far as nude parades were concerned, and rumour had it that there would be serious repercussions if they paraded naked into town.

One nice summer afternoon we received word that a Doukhobor nude parade was heading south out of Veregin on No. 5 highway, heading towards Kamsack. It was estimated there were eighty to a hundred people in the parade, of both sexes and all ages, and all completely naked. We immediately took off for Veregin and intercepted the parade about two miles south of town. Other patrols soon arrived on the scene with various trucks and buses. Our job was to get the nude protesters into trucks and drive them to Yorkton for a court appearance.

We had trouble loading these people in the trucks. None offered any physical resistance but were completely impassive, most difficult to handle. I recall I was trying to persuade, load, shove, or push a very large Doukhobor lady weighing about 250 pounds onto a stool and thus into the back of the truck. She was most uncooperative and so I wasn't making much progress. It was a very warm, humid day and the naked women were perspiring freely. My lady friend seemed to be enjoying my efforts.

I looked across to the next truck. There was my sidekick, Matt, with a very comely teenage girl. He was smiling a lot and not trying very hard to get her into the truck. He looked over at me, winked, and said, "Imagine, Joe, they're *paying* us for this!"

9

VERBAL CARNAGE

God don't make no mistakes.
That's how He got to be God.
— Archie Bunker

Laughter, that great elixir, often erupts in gloomy courtrooms because certain people don't know the meaning of certain words, and this causes them to butcher said words, and sometimes even sacred rules of grammar, beyond all recognition.

Such calamities also occur fairly often in police work, I'm pleased to report.

——————————

Sergeant Les Weir of the Ontario Provincial Police in Petrolia sent me a "short but true" story, which he tells as follows:

Recently our regular court officer, whose name is Jack, called in sick and had to be temporarily replaced by another officer. During one of the recesses a fellow court officer, a woman genuinely interested in Jack's whereabouts, asked the replacement court officer, in a relatively loud voice in a quiet but crowded courtroom, "Jack off today?"

The witty pinch-hitter, in an equally loud voice, quickly responded, "Not today, but I did twice last week."

• • •

"Typo-itis" is a highly contagious disease that afflicts countless folks, including cops and wannabe cops, of course.

For example, fingerprint forms received at the head office of the RCMP sometimes contain peculiar typing errors. One came from the "Director of Navel Intelligence, Navel Hdqrs., Ottawa." Another form warned, "The following information snot supported." came from "Fancouver, B.C." and reported that the defendant discussed therein had been found "not quilty."

• • •

Back in the 1950s, the RCMP encouraged young men to write essays on why they wanted to be Mounties. These literary efforts were judged by high-ranking members of the force and led to the enlistment of many promising new policemen.

When the judges saw one particular essay they wondered whose side the applicant was on. It read in part: "The Royal Canadian Mounted Police could quite readily be defined as the 'World's Most Famous Police Corpse.'"

• • •

I received an interesting letter from Charles M. Bauer of Ottawa, who was a justice of the peace in St. Boniface, Manitoba, from 1953 to 1967. He still chuckles when he recalls an entry made by a francophone in the lost-and-found register of the

St. Boniface Police Department:
"Found: a pair of testicles, gold-rimmed."

• • •

Crown counsel Steve Stirling of Port Alberni, British Columbia, reports that in a case he once prosecuted a policeman issued a traffic ticket for "carless driving."

• • •

Errors in police reports are fairly common, like this one from San Diego: "When Sergeant Peck responded to a radio call about a dog locked in a closed car on a hot day, he quickly typed a message and asked that Animal Control respond to a dog suffering from 'heat prostitution.'"

• • •

A few years ago an item in the San Diego Police Department's newsletter, *Up Front*, read: "A Public Affairs sergeant who shall remain nameless wrote an internal memo about potential donations for a worthy cause which said that 'the Department would put the money into a centralized suppository.' Now you know where all the money has gone."

• • •

Slips of the tongue sometimes pop out of the mouths of police officers testifying in court.

Court reporter Jack Gordon of Hanover, Ontario, recalls the time he recorded the evidence in an impaired-driving prosecution brought against a woman. The investigating officer rattled off the usual signs of impairment — glassy eyes, slurred speech, unsteady gait — and added that "there was a smell of liquor on her breast."

• • •

Screwed-up syntax can knock a sentence out of kilter, with

disastrous and often humorous results. And it's downright sinful what some cops do with their syntax.

For instance, in an impaired driving case in Saskatchewan a police officer who was preparing a report for the prosecutor left this pip for posterity:

"Constable Gamble, the Breathalyzer technician, noted a very strong smell of liquor with a Ukrainian-type accent."

• • •

And from a report prepared by a British Columbia police officer:

"April 23, 1980 — observed subject sit stationary at 3rd Avenue and Angus at a high rate of speed."

• • •

In a court in Ireland early in this century, a policeman testified: "He rode a bicycle the worse for liquor, without a light, and smelling strongly of drink."

• • •

In preparing a report about an accident involving a car and a bicycle, an RCMP officer wrote that the bike was "equipped with a headlight, rear red reflector, and believed to be in an inebriated condition."

• • •

While reporting a case in which a man was charged with causing a disturbance in a public place, another Mountie wrote:

"As a result of a phone call that a fight was taking place in the café, a patrol was made and the accused was found trying to fight with anybody in general and hit a person in a booth, who was eating his supper for no apparent reason whatsoever."

• • •

In yet another RCMP case, this little dilly leapt out of a report pertaining to a man charged with driving his truck without having the required clearance lights on it:

"The accused appeared in court with the necessary number of required clearance lights attached and in working order."

• • •

Several years ago a San Diego policeman wrote in a report that "a man alleged he'd been stabbed by his wife during an argument with a large kitchen knife."

Which inspired a waggish colleague to note: "The moral is, never argue with a kitchen knife. They lack empathy."

• • •

Say, what *is* it with San Diego? A police officer in that syntax-shattered city ended an assault report with these wacky words:

"I took a photograph of the victim showing the injuries to his head, which is attached to the detective's copy."

• • •

One day in 1988 a policeman in Fort Worth, Texas, dashed off a crime report for the District Attorney's office, one sentence of which read thusly: "The man entered the laundromat, grabbed the woman's breast, and fled."

Quipped assistant D.A. Cindy Singleton: "We didn't know whether to charge the man with disorderly conduct, theft, or desecration of a venerated object."

• • •

An Edmonton, Alberta, policeman filed this snappy report:

A dispatcher sent two constables out to a suburban area of the city after a woman called in to ask that police (her words) "prevent a breach of the peace while I pick up my horse."

This prompted one of the officers to remark, "If she can pick up a horse, she doesn't need us."

• • •

The confusion continues unabated — confusion created by mystifying words that leave bewildered readers or listeners shaking their heads and muttering, "Huh?" If you don't know what makes them tick, words can blow up in your face — as we're about to see.

RCMP Constable Jack MacNeill, of Charlottetown, Prince Edward Island, filed this report on behalf of a colleague:

One summer, during the annual rotation of personnel, Constable Bruce MacDonald was showing a new and rather naive member around the area. While making the rounds they encountered a local man who was so wild in his younger days he'd been given a frontal lobotomy in an institution in Alberta.

Bruce pointed out the unfortunate fellow and told the young officer, "That's the only person I've ever seen who was given a frontal lobotomy."

The new member, who shall remain nameless, replied, "No shit, does he still have it?"

• • •

Justine Adamek, a policewoman you met in chapter four, returns with a story about a mental lapse she had while on duty:

I'm twenty-six years old and have been with the Australian Federal Police in Canberra for seven years. I don't think I'm very naive. However, the other day I was called to go to a burglary that had been committed in what's known as a light industrial estate — an area where technical, mechanical, electrical and home-improvement businesses are located. These areas are also renowned for housing "love shops" and massage parlours.

Anyway, off I trotted to investigate a burglary at a place called Sweet Affaire. Of course, it didn't even occur to me that I was looking for a massage parlour. I kept driving around looking for a chocolate shop!

• • •

Sometimes the confusion we speak of here is caused by one party not listening to the other. An Alberta court reporter, Robin Grigat, sent me this dab of courtroom dialogue between a lawyer and a cop who must have had a wad of wax in his ears:

Q. And did you bear arms, Constable?
A. Yes, it was a short-sleeved shirt.
Q. I'm sorry. Were you carrying a weapon?
A. No, I was not. I had no side arms on, no, but I had bare arms.

• • •

Lieutenant Colonel D. Brian Murphy, of Ottawa, supplied me with a partial transcript of a Canadian military trial in which a military policeman testified. A snippet reads as follows:

Q. Officer, what position was the defendant in while he was being searched?
A. He had two hands on the wall, sir, and two on the ground.

• • •

Sometimes folks are pulverized by words — especially if they have no idea of their meaning. Arthur Slaght, the top criminal lawyer in Toronto in the 1930s, kayoed the chief Crown witness with a few fast verbal jabs in a drunk-driving case.

"After the accident, was the accused verbose?" Slaght asked the investigating police officer.

"I don't understand your question," the policeman replied.

189

"Did he talk a lot?"

"No."

"Was he lachrymose?"

"Pardon me?"

"Did he cry?"

"No."

"Was the accused bellicose?"

"Huh?"

"Did he want to fight?"

"Uh, no."

"Was he comatose?"

"What does that mean?"

"Was he asleep?"

"No."

"Your Honour," said Slaght, "I have no further questions. This witness doesn't know *anything*!"

After the jurors had stopped laughing they acquitted the accused.

● ● ●

Anyone who's ever heard police officers testifying in court would likely be interested in the comments of a judge of the Federal Court of Appeals in the 1976 case of *United States* v. *Marshall*. Calling attention to the stilted manner in which federal agents (he could have added, "and many other policemen") give their testimony, His Honour stated for the record:

"The agents involved speak an almost impenetrable jargon. They do not get into their cars; they enter official government vehicles. They do not get out of or leave their cars; they exit them. They do not go somewhere; they proceed. They do not go to a particular place; they proceed to its vicinity. They do not watch or look; they surveille. They never see anything; they observe it. No one tells them anything; they are advised. A person does not tell them his name; he identifies himself. A person does not say something; he indicates. They do not listen to a telephone conversation; they monitor it.

"People telephoning each other do not say hello; they exchange greetings. An agent does not hand money to an informer to make a buy; he advances previously recorded official government funds. To an agent, a list of serial numbers does not list serial numbers; it depicts Federal Reserve Notes. An agent does not say what an exhibit is; he says what it purports to be. The agents preface answers to simple and direct questions with 'to my knowledge.' They cannot describe a conversation by saying 'he said' and 'I said'; they speak in conclusions. Sometimes it takes the combined efforts of counsel and the judge to get them to state who said what."

• • •

The Honourable Allan McEachern, Chief Justice of British Columbia, recently sent me a specimen of copspeak from a trial he presided at. It seems a young RCMP officer was giving evidence that he and other officers were in the living room of a dwelling. When the witness was asked what he did next, he replied, "I went on a patrol into the kitchen."

• • •

We're embarking now on a patrol of our own — a journey into the wonderfully wacky world of a couple of funny fellows named MacDonald. In case I'm suspected of indulging in nepotism, I swear that I've never met either of these now-deceased entertainers, nor am I related to either one of them.

Hughie R. MacDonald and Angus "Blue" MacDonald hailed from Cape Breton, a part of Nova Scotia that has always teemed with colourful characters and natural-born storytellers, a region that has spawned a slew of honest-to-God living legends.

Plenty of people are locally famous for a spell, but living legends are folks who are celebrated in story and sometimes in song, as well, long before — and long *after* — they've gone to their eternal reward. In the first half of this century, in a small area of Cape Breton alone, there were at least three men who met these criteria. One was Magistrate A.B. MacGillivray, whose forty-seven-year "reign" in Glace Bay was traced in my first book, *Court Jesters*. The other two happen to be our honoured guests — Hughie R. MacDonald, of Sydney, and Angus "Blue" MacDonald, of Glace Bay.

Hugh Ranald MacDonald, known as Hughie R. throughout his sixty-plus years on this planet, was born and raised at West Bay, Inverness County, in the early 1900s. He left school when he was still a lad, and for quite a few years thereafter he worked on the family farm. When he was in his twenties he chucked agriculture and journeyed some seventy miles to the smallish city of Sydney, where he joined the police force.

"Hughie R. was typical of the kind of policeman that was prevalent in the area up to about 1960," says Sydney lawyer David N. Muise, who knows a lot about the subject. "He was big and strong, like most of the cops who came from the country. That's just what police forces wanted — big, burly cops who could subdue anyone who caused trouble. They didn't care if a job-seeker left school in grade six, and they were glad if he could converse in Gaelic, which was a snap for lots of rural fellows.

"It's hard to believe in this day and age," David continues, "but a few decades ago the Sydney Police Department did much of its dispatching in Gaelic. There were so many country boys on the force that the dispatcher could give messages in Gaelic and they wouldn't have to worry about anyone intercepting their communications."

Alex Goldie dropped out of school in grade five, but it didn't stop him from joining the Sydney police force in 1941 and becoming its chief in 1973.

"Hughie was built like a brick shed from feet to head," Goldie told me. "He was six feet tall and weighed about 280 pounds. He had black hair and his thick face was always very red. He was a good policeman and an awfully powerful man. If he got you in a bear hug he could squeeze you to death."

The public perception is that Hughie R. was a big lovable boob who just couldn't help saying really dumb things that got really big laughs for those who kept recycling them — still a popular activity three decades after his death. But there are those who knew him who say he was actually quite bright and enjoyed the limelight.

No matter how you look at it, though, generations of folks are deeply indebted to Hughie for bringing them the blessed balm of laughter. Let's examine some evidence.

The best-known — and most-repeated — Hughie R. tale was triggered by the sudden demise of a pony on a downtown Sydney street called The Esplanade. Police regulations required the cop on the beat to compose a detailed report on the grave event, including where it happened. The cop on the beat was Hughie R. MacDonald, who realized immediately that he had a hell of a problem on his hands, namely, how do you spell Esplanade?

Legend has it that, responding to a brain wave, Hughie dragged the pony two hundred feet to Pitt Street, which he knew how to spell, and then made out his report.

"True," a Sydney old-timer tells me, "and he even spelled Pitt incorrectly."

• • •

Another dandy tale relates to the sticky subject of spelling.

One day, the story goes, Constable MacDonald flagged down a motorist for going through a stop sign and then stuck his huge head into the car and growled:

"That sign said S-T-O-P, not S-L-O."

• • •

Mounting evidence suggests that Hughie R. was mighty confused about the *meaning* of a good many words, too. We have David N. Muise to thank for this short, snappy story:

Hughie once charged a well-known street woman with arson. When asked why he did this, he replied, "Because she's been arsin' around on Charlotte Street for years."

• • •

Just when you're convinced Hughie R. MacDonald had absolutely no feel for words, you're pleasantly surprised.

Alex Goldie told me about a case he worked on with Hughie in the early 1940s. A Sydney man whose last name was Laffin had disappeared under mysterious circumstances, and the city police were alerted. One day they received a report that someone had seen the body of a man lying facedown in the creek at Wentworth Park. Hughie and Goldie hustled to the scene.

Goldie, who knew the man they were looking for, turned the body upright and said, "This man is Laffin."

"He's not laughin," quipped Hughie, "he's *dead!*"

When I spoke to the former Sydney police chief in late 1994, I was delighted to receive official confirmation of one of Hughie R.'s most famous utterances. Alex Goldie, who was in his thirties at the time, said he was standing about three feet behind the much older Sergeant MacDonald when the latter unleashed the line that caused generations of fun-loving folks to giggle and guffaw. The story goes like this:

One day in the late-1940s, Hughie R. arrested a woman for being drunk and disorderly in a public place. Seconds after he put her in the slammer, she sang out, "Oh, Officer, I'll need Kotex in the morning," and Hughie R. snarled, "Aw, shut up, you'll have Corn Flakes like the rest of them!"

• • •

Before introducing our second guest of honour, Angus "Blue" MacDonald, a few preliminary remarks are in order.

Angus was never a cop — not officially, that is. But as a long-time member of the Glace Bay Town Council, he was automatically a longtime member of the Glace Bay Police Commission, and that made him a longtime important part of the local police scene.

Hughie and Angus knew each other, and their stamping grounds were only ten miles apart, but apparently they never did a gig together. However, it's pretty plain that though Hughie murdered the mother tongue masterfully, and always to the tune of very loud laughter, when it came to committing linguistic mayhem Angus Blue MacDonald was — thank God! — in a class by himself. Hordes of folks who either heard the maestro's humdingers in person or got them via the grapevine are eternally grateful to him for all the chuckles he sent their way.

For some reason no one's been able to explain to me, Angus's family has long been known in the Glace Bay area as "the Blue MacDonalds," and so, in accordance with the age-old Cape Breton method of quickly identifying families by nick-names, their children and their children's children and their children's children's children, will likely always have "Blue" in their name. For example, two of Angus's children have been known all their lives as Archie Blue and Joe Blue.

Without further ado I present herewith a medley of Angus Blue's all-time biggest hits.

• • •

Back in the 1940s Glace Bay councillors debated whether or not the town should purchase and install an extremely fancy and expensive chandelier to pretty up the council chambers. Some of the local politicians favoured the idea and some were "agin" it.

Councillor Angus Blue MacDonald was adamantly opposed, stating that the project was an unnecessary venture and far too costly for the town's rather puny purse.

"And, besides," he added, "nobody in Glace Bay can play one of those damn things, anyway."

• • •

On another memorable occasion Glace Bay Town Council decided to purchase six Japanese pagodas, at a cost of two thousand dollars a pagoda, to decorate Queen Elizabeth Park. The lone dissenter was Angus Blue, who didn't have the faintest idea what a pagoda was.

Angus told his legislative colleagues that the price mentioned was far too steep, but he said he might be able to go for some sort of compromise.

"Like what?" one of the councillors asked him.

"Well," he said, "why don't we just buy two — a boy pagoda and a girl pagoda — and mate them?"

• • •

David Muise, the source for some of the Hughie R. MacDonald tales, has a few gems about Angus Blue, too. He told me this one:

In the baby-boom days of the 1950s, the Glace Bay schools were very overcrowded. Old schools were quite run-down and some of the parents and teachers were bugging town councillors (who were also the school board) to do some renovations if they couldn't build new schools.

Angus Blue decided to pay a visit to one particular school to view the washrooms. There was a dire need for more facilities there because of the increased numbers of children, especially little boys. Teachers wanted the school board to put in more urinals.

At the next meeting of the board Angus Blue recommended that the members authorize the purchase and installation of six urinals. "And since there's girls going there, too," he added, "you should also get a few more arsenals."

• • •

For decades, the town council dealt with endless problems that were caused when ruptured sewer mains swept raw sewage into Renwick Brook and thence into Glace Bay Harbour. During one of the many council debates on this sordid subject, an exasperated Angus told council members he was "extremely concerned about affluence breaking out in our community."

• • •

My brother, Alan MacDonald, of Calgary, Alberta, passed on this wonderful Angus Blue pronouncement: "The trouble with the Liberal Party of Nova Scotia is that they don't know how to get down to the brass roots."

• • •

Angus "Blue" MacDonald was a proud and busy member of the Canadian Legion. He once attended a national meeting of that august organization, at which delegates debated whether to publish the *Legionnaire* magazine in English and French. Angus made a rousing speech — replete with butchered words, mangled metaphors, and other linguistic atrocities — in which he supported the idea of publishing in both languages.

He was followed by a speaker from Quebec, who thanked him very much and then added a nice little touch by formally moving that the magazine be published "in English and French — and whatever language that last speaker spoke in."

10

CRITTERS

Animals are such agreeable friends — they ask no questions, they pass no criticisms.
— George Eliot

I agree with the foregoing in most cases. But our furry friends sometimes get into situations that can leave us humans cackling with laughter or ripping hair out of our skulls — or both.

Our first informant is Inspector Eric Fiander of the Criminal Investigation Division of the Fredericton Police Force, in New Brunswick. He's anxious to tell us about his friend Sparky, a cuddly canine who helped solve a serious crime.

"Sparky wasn't a bad dog," Inspector Fiander says for starters. "The company he kept, however, left a lot to be desired. Sparky, a pert little beagle mix, loved to walk. Sparky's owner loved to walk his dog in quiet neighbourhoods, where the pickings for break and enter were ripe." Inspector Fiander gives us the rest of the story:

CID investigator Michael Richard responded to a request from patrol personnel that he go to the scene of a residential break and enter in late March of 1993. An elderly couple had vacationed in sunnier climes and when they returned they found their home ransacked.

The MO of this break resembled numerous other reported incidents during the past several weeks. Investigator Richard asked the couple who fed the dog while they were away. They said they didn't have a dog.

Richard took a closer look and, yes, those were dog pawprints on the couch. The identification unit was summoned to the scene, and they vacuumed the couch and recovered several short dark-brown hairs. A few days later Richard showed up in the booking office with a man in custody. Also "in custody" was Sparky the Dog, who was "seized" as evidence.

A mournful and frightened Sparky was placed in a solid-door cell so he couldn't escape through the bars while his master was interviewed. A short time later the human suspect was placed in a cell while Sparky was taken out for a combing. Hair was pulled and combed from the dog to be sent to the crime lab for analysis and comparison with the hair recovered on the couch.

Sparky was paraded around the CID before being placed back in his cell. It was decided that, as a joke on the investigator, Sparky should be pawprinted and photographed for the record. Sparky and his owner were released later that day and were given a court date for a few weeks down the road.

Early the next morning Inspector Fiander opened the door to his office and called loudly for Richard. Seconds later the two of them were admiring a huge pile of dog droppings on the inspector's carpet. As he went to clean up this mess, Mike Richard discovered that the droppings were a very realistic rubber, and this caused great glee among the chaps in CID.

In December 1993, at the CID Christmas party, Richard was presented with a plaque bearing a picture of Sparky, as well as a generous supply of rubber dog droppings and a flea collar. The plaque bore the inscription, "Collar of the Year, 1993."

"And what became of Sparky? His master pleaded guilty, largely because the hairs taken from his dog proved that the accused was at the scene of the crime, and so Sparky wasn't required to give any further evidence.

Sparky and his owner live about a block from a liquor store, and word has it that the dog has been seen hanging around the parking lot of said emporium. Some say Sparky may have taken to drink. That's another story, and I'm not one to spread stories about lovable, law-abiding beagles.

• • •

Police dogs never cease to amaze their masters, and many others who happen to see them in action. A few years ago an anonymous cop wrote this report and preserved it for posterity in the San Diego Police Department's newsletter, *Up Front*:

Sgt. Shockley and Sgt. Santi were involved in a pursuit (vehicle) that started in Southeast (precinct) and ended at 52 and Contour, where the suspect bailed into a canyon. Sgt. Shockley tripped over a wire and fell down. The suspect was taken into custody without incident. During his tumble down the hill, Sgt. Shockley lost his badge. He requested the Canine Unit to check for his badge.

I checked the area and saw that it was very unstable ground with thick bushes over it. I didn't think Dax [the police dog] could get into the brush without falling. I sent him into the bushes from the fastest point of entry several times. He seemed more concerned about his footing than his searching.

I did not see him search or sniff for anything. I did not think he was searching, so I took him back to my car. When he got to the car, I told him to get in. He looked at me, spat out the badge, and got into the car.

• • •

Critters sometimes find themselves in the weirdest situations — even on the highway. Retired physician Lois Pearce, of Chatham, Ontario, narrates a story that still makes her laugh fifty years after she first heard it:

Soon after the Second World War, a Dr. Phogg came from England and set up practice in Sault Ste. Marie, Ontario, bringing with him his tiny canvas-roofed two-seater English car with right-hand drive. Dr. Phogg may have had many sterling qualities, but good bookkeeping was not his forte, and he was rather more fond of alcoholic beverages than some could approve.

One half-holiday he was studying his accounts and noticed that a farmer in the Echo Bay area had an appreciable debt on which he had made no payments. Dr. Phogg decided that it would be a good idea to call on the man and ask him to start making payments on his bill.

The farmer greeted the doctor enthusiastically, stating that he'd just been thinking he should be making payments on the account owing. Then he said that Dr. Phogg had arrived at a most propitious moment and he might be willing to help him make some important decisions. He'd been making wine, and he thought it *might* be ready to be bottled. Could the good doctor help him decide? The good doctor could.

It turned out to be a rather difficult decision to make, for there were several batches of wine to be considered. The two men spent the rest of the afternoon and part of the evening carefully tasting and deciding. Eventually they had not only decided what to do with the wine, but Dr. Phogg had happily accepted a nanny goat in total payment of the man's debt.

Dr. Phogg and his paid-up patient got the goat loaded into the passenger seat of the little English car and set out for home. The wine had a rather bad effect on the doctor's driving (poor Phogg was in a fog) and he found it quite impossible to keep the car on a proper course.

A rookie policeman was on patrol with a senior officer acting as his mentor. They stopped Dr. Phogg and the young cop stepped up to the car, prepared to make his first arrest. He went to what he presumed was the driver's side of the vehicle and found himself face-to-face with a nanny goat who appeared to be the driver of the car.

It took a while to sort that one out.

• • •

Constable Greg Ferguson, who served with the RCMP in Hampton, New Brunswick, and now works at Customs and Excise in Saint John, tells of a horribly harried heifer:

An Udder Disaster

On a bright sunny but cold New Brunswick day at Hampton detachment, I was sitting in the office when I received a call from a local resident stating that there was a loose cow running down the Hall Road in the village of Hampton.

You must realize that the village of Hampton is bordered by the river on one side and Highway 1 on the other. Since there were no farms in this area, I had to presume that the cow either crossed the river or a very busy highway.

As I drove to the scene, Corporal Bob Gallup and Constable Wayne White were in hotfoot pursuit of the rather large cow, which appeared larger as one got closer.

At first the cow was herded into a semifenced back yard. Not liking the scenery too much, she decided to visit every back yard for a two-block radius, which made matters worse. As local motorists saw us from the various streets, they would usually blow their horns, which would make the cow crazy and send her running in any direction.

The chase lasted for approximately three miles, which covered numerous back yards, a railway track, a frozen river (guess what we were hoping), and, if you can believe this, the local butcher shop.

As the unhappy heifer was travelling in the direction of two elementary schools and a junior high school, it was time for drastic action. Constable White, having watched many hours of WWF wrestling, decided to put the dreaded ultimate warrior headlock on the cow. Both White and our four-legged friend were in full flight. I had every intention of doing the same thing, but after a half-second I thought, "*Nah.*"

Anyway, White jumped the cow in the middle of the street. The cow took off over a snowbank about five feet high and then down the other side, White hanging off her and being thrown around like a rag doll. They went into a church yard with White still holding on.

About a quarter of the way into the parking lot, several other civilians lent a hand and the cow was placed under arrest. I couldn't help hold the cow, because I was reading her the Charter Notice, Police Warning, and Secondary Warning, and it took some time to get the various cards out of my briefcase in the car, three miles away.

The cow was tied to a telephone pole while the owner was rounded up. When he arrived he took one look at the cow and decided he'd better summon a vet to give her a shot, as she was still pretty unhappy about matters.

The vet arrived and gave the cow one cc of some drug. One cc didn't look like much to me. However, the vet assured me several times that this would do the trick. The cow received the shot and about fifteen minutes later she seemed drunk and was herded into the truck. (I was back in the car looking for an

Appearance Notice to serve on the accused animal.)

A couple of valuable lessons were learned by this city boy: (1) Content cows are seen and not chased, and (2) Body-slamming Hulk Hogan would be easier than tussling with a thousand-pound cow.

• • •

And speaking of cows . . . Meet Professor S. Venugopal Rao, who for more than four decades has been closely associated with the Indian Police Service, first as a police officer and later as a researcher and writer in the field of criminology. In his autobiography, *Baton and the Pen*, he reminisces about the time the almighty Deputy Inspector General (DIG for short) came to inspect a small-town police station he was running. This sort of thing occurred often in Indian police circles, and it was customary to shower the DIG with goodies and perks and treat him as if he were royalty. On this occasion, Murphy's Law ran amok.

In the early evening Rao was told that the DIG and his wife would be arriving at about 8:00 p.m., and he was told to meet them at the "traveller's bungalow" — police rest house — and spoil them rotten.

"Please ensure that men are posted at all important road diversions to ensure that the DIG does not lose his way," Rao was instructed. "You know that town of yours — once he goes into a wrong alley, he's lost."

It struck Rao that an important feature was lost sight of. If the dignitary was arriving at 8:00 p.m., it meant that dinner had to be arranged. Rao mentioned this to his worthy superior.

"Ah! I was wondering when you'd come to that," the man replied with a grunt of satisfaction. "There will be no need for dinner, but *there must be enough milk.*"

"Milk!" Rao exclaimed in surprise."

"Yes, m-i-l-k," his boss spelled out to avoid any further confusion. "I am surprised that you do not know that these are days of fasting for the DIG. For religious reasons, he does not take anything but milk at night."

Rao waited and waited for the exalted guest to arrive. Finally, about 11:00 p.m., he saw headlights bobbing on the road and a car turning into the rest-house grounds. He dashed across the road and greeted the DIG. The man was curt and seemed to be under some strain, but he managed to say, affably enough, "We were delayed. You may come here tomorrow about ten when we can go to the police station for inspection."

In the middle of the night Rao was wakened by a screechy car horn and an insistent knocking on the door. He jumped out of bed and opened the door.

The Superintendent of Police was standing there, an angry God, raining curses on the Inspector and the Sub-Inspector, who were cowering behind him. Rao led him into his drawing room and asked him what had upset him.

The Superintendent was furious because nothing had gone right.

"The DIG was delayed," he said, "but the man you posted at the road junction to give a proper direction deserted his post. He says he stayed put till about 11:00 p.m., even though he was under extreme discomfort, and had just moved to answer the calls of nature. When he saw the dazzling lights of the car, he could not come back like that, could he? It was at that moment that the car took the wrong turn . . ."

"Still," Rao said, "there should have been no problem."

"That's the most unfortunate part of it," his superior bemoaned. "In one of the alleys the car stalled. Our DIG and his son had to push it a long way before it started."

The Superintendent began to tell Rao some do's and dont's of police work.

"Senior officers should personally supervise and check everything," he said. "Never leave it to the subordinates, who have an incredible propensity for mismanaging even the simplest of chores. It's disgraceful that, despite my clear instructions, *there was no milk!*"

"No milk!" Rao exclaimed in consternation. "I was assured by the Inspector and the Sub-Inspector that they had made fool-proof arrangements!"

"Our dithering fools think they are clever," his boss exploded. "They brought a cow and tethered it behind the traveller's bungalow, with a milkman in attendance, ready to milk the cow as soon as the DIG arrrived. But when there was an inordinate delay, the milkman fell asleep and the cow's thirsty calf helped itself to the milk — every last drop of it."

• • •

Radio operator Fred Sauve, of the Ontario Provincial Police detachment in North Bay, recalls a caper he was involved in when he was stationed in Haileybury:

Early one Sunday morning, I received a report of a cow on Highway 558, just west of the Haileybury detachment. Constable Cliff Hallworth, a great kidder, was dispatched to round up this bovine before it got hit by a motorist.

After sending Cliff to this call, I didn't hear from him for nearly an hour. Wondering what was taking him so long, I called to ask him how things were going, and how much longer he thought it would take him to get clear from this occurrence.

Hallworth broke me up when he replied, "If this bull doesn't get out of this cow, I'll be here the whole damn day!"

• • •

In the not-so-merrie England of the early 1800s, Lord Palmerston, later prime minister of Great Britain, once remarked, "The best thing for the inside of a man is the outside of a horse." And a generation later the budding British prime minister Benjamin Disraeli stated ever so categorically, "A canter is the cure for every evil."

Well, we're about to meet a couple of fellows who accumulated a lot of evidence to the contrary.

The first is retired RCMP Sergeant A. "Scotty" Wallace of Midland, Ontario, who describes a memorable adventure he had at Mountie training school in Regina, Saskatchewan, circa 1930:

Many years ago at Regina I was one of several eager beavers being taught the rudiments of horsemanship. We had, I remember, a Cockney riding instructor who, being an expert rider, was also extremely proficient in the use of a certain vocabulary.

At any rate, we were out at the riding school one day astride our steeds, sitting prim and proper, stiff as ramrods, when we got the command, "Right leg ovah!" This meant taking our feet out of the stirrups, lifting the right leg over the horse's neck, and coming to a sitting position facing away from the horse's left side. We sat there as before, to all appearances stiff as pokers, but if the other lads were anything like myself, this outward appearance was only a camouflage for insides like jelly.

Jelly, as the whole world knows, should be allowed to settle, but ours didn't get that chance, for in no time we got the further command, "Left leg ovah!" I'll leave you to figure out which way we were facing then. Somehow the world looks entirely different from a horse's rear end. You feel, so to speak, as if you're at a loose end, no control over anything, let come what may.

It did, for in a moment's carelessness I allowed my spurs to tickle my four-legged keg of dynamite, and away we went, hell-bent for election. Don't ask me whither. I was aware only of the world receding at an alarming rate and the voice of an irate instructor shouting, "Take your spurs out of that blankety-blank horse!" I was hanging on for dear life, clutching anything and everything. I would even have used my teeth, only I'm not too partial to rump steak.

But, as with all things, there has to be an end. In this case it happened to be *my* end, because the dear little beastie came to a sudden stop and I described the loveliest arc you ever saw, right over its head — only I did it in reverse, a sort of double loop with a one-point landing in the brush. Amidst the thorns, the chagrin, and the pain, I remember looking up into a pair of docile, disinterested eyes. For all the animal cared I might as well have not existed — and when the instructor finished with me I wished I hadn't.

• • •

The other chap who'll show us the reverse side of the coin is Ed McPhail of Milton, Ontario, a retired inspector with the Ontario Provincial Police who also served for a spell with the Mounties:

While training with the RCMP in Regina, young recruits were privileged to meet a truly compassionate riding instructor by the name of Corporal Harry Armstrong.

One of Harry's finer moments occurred during a lane-jumping exercise one hot summer day in 1956. A lane approximately fifteen feet wide and enclosed by two boards on wooden posts contained three jumps. The rider would cross his stirrups, tie off the reins, fold his arms and streak down the lane, attempting to tip his hat to the instructor while negotiating each jump.

On the day in question, one unfortunate fellow was thrown from his horse sideways through a two-by-four and onto the sun-baked prairie clay, sustaining a broken shoulder blade as well as losing all breath from his body.

Harry, compassion oozing from every pore, looked down at the recruit and inquired in his deep voice, "Constable, who told you to dismount?"

• • •

In 1990 ex-RCMP officer Jack White published this piece in an anthology of Mountie memories, *The Way It Was.*

The Cougar Caper

At the turn of the century, Golden, British Columbia, had been a boom town with mills, bars, and a house of ill repute running twenty-four hours a day. By the time I got there in the fifties the mills had slowed, the bars were gone, and an old weather-worn house on the edge of town gave little hint of stories past obtained from old court-record books on our back-room shelves. The single occupant was a quiet and frail little old lady, now in the twilight of her years, who kept to herself and bothered no one.

Her visit to our office one day was a surprise in itself, but more so when the nature of her problem unfolded. She was being threatened by cougars. Cougars are a naturally shy and cautious animal, so it came as no surprise when none were sighted and she was safely delivered home and cautioned to make a prompt telephone call to the local game warden if another should appear.

Within the day our office received another visitor in the presence of the game warden himself to advise he had just come from a cougar scare. Yes, it was the same place and again none were found.

Over the following days we took turns answering more frequent summonses, finally coming to the slow realization that the cougars bore a strong hint of imagination about them. From our view, an imaginary cougar posed an even bigger problem; it was increasingly evident that our little old lady was perhaps half a bubble out of plumb, which meant a committal to a mental institution. That meant almost twenty-four hours on escort by train to Vancouver with a little old lady whose frail condition left one to wonder if she would even survive the trip.

The corporal, the game warden, and I went to the local restaurant for refreshments and consultation over a cup of coffee. The relaxed atmosphere produced results. Someone (not me) came up with the bright idea that if we shot the cougars, maybe the problem would disappear. The more it was joked about, the more plausible it became. Soon three pairs of eager hands were removing slugs from revolver cartridges. After all, a blank should suitably dispatch an imaginary cougar, and it would make a suitable noise and provide no risk to the surroundings.

With due alacrity and now suitably armed, the three of us in full uniform arrived at the scene. The complainant answered our knock and seemed most relieved that we had come. In answer to our request, she volunteered to show us where the dangerous animals usually lay in wait about her yard. Almost at once, she pointed directly behind us to where one was even now surely advancing.

Turning as one, with revolvers at the ready, we found ourselves confronted by a very menacing tuft of grass! Seeking reassurance, the corporal turned a questioning glance at our complainant. "Shoot him!" she said. Accordingly he fired, and she gleefully exclaimed, "You got him!"

When the smoke cleared away after several more shots, she finally said, "Thank you so much, you've got them all." At this point I beat a hasty but discreet retreat to the police car to give vent to the hysterics I could feel rising — imagine grown men, and in uniform, shooting shrubbery! I was called back to remove the bodies. I just couldn't go through with that pretence, but I did hold the trunk lid open while the other two dutifully hoisted the invisible carcasses into the trunk.

At last they were loaded, doors slammed, and we set off, convulsed with laughter. We came to a screeching halt after travelling only a few yards. Wondering why, I looked back to see the little old lady frantically waving. "We must have missed one," someone joked as the corporal put the car in reverse. Rolling down his window, the game warden asked, "Yes, what is it?"

"I was just wondering," she said, "who's going to get the bounty?"

11

Some of This, Some of That

Variety's the very spice of life,
That gives it all its flavour.
— William Cowper

Do you like variety? Boy, have we got variety . . .

Constable Jack MacNeill of the RCMP detachment in Charlottetown, Prince Edward Island, relates this ripsnorting story about some police colleagues:

Prior to joining the RCMP, Constable Scott Lundrigan worked for a period with the city police of Halifax, Nova Scotia. On the evening of July 1, 1988 — Canada's 121st birthday — Lundrigan and Constable Jamie Simonson were patrolling the steep slopes of historic Citadel Hill. While so doing, they encountered a pair of extremely drunk and belligerent sailors. After a strenuous scuffle the officers were able to handcuff the troublemakers' hands behind their backs, then prop both men up against a wrought-iron fence and start to frisk them.

This fence, on the east side of the Hill, is quite high above the sidewalk, and only a suicidal maniac or a drunken sailor on leave would consider jumping the fence from such a height. And that's exactly what Lundrigan's prisoner did. He leaned over the fence and executed a complete forward somersault over the rail and fell ten feet to the sidewalk below, where, incredibly enough, he landed on his feet and began to run like hell.

Lundrigan, still dazed by the spectacular escape and knowing that to pursue the fellow in the same fashion would be highly dangerous, began to consider what he'd say to his superiors about "the one that got away." Then an amazing thing happened.

The fleeing sailor had taken only a few strides when, out of the darkness, came a swift straight-arm that brought him crashing to the ground.

As the officers peered over the railing to see who their guardian angel was, they saw a burly man walking along and looking up at them with a grin. Then they heard the fellow say without breaking stride, "Bernie Schwartz — New York Police Department — on vacation — glad to be of assistance." And then he vanished into the night.

• • •

Police officers run the risk of being mowed down by a hail of bullets — or perhaps a shower of kisses. When Tony Krings, of Scarborough, Ontario, left his native Germany and emigrated to Canada in 1954, he brought lots of true, funny police stories with him. One pertained to a pleasant sort of excitement experienced annually by hordes of cops in his homeland:

Karnival is a most happy time, especially in my hometown, Cologne, on the Rhine. Some people will do anything to participate in the fun — even taking their bed to the pawnshop to have money for the many events.

Thursday before Karnival's Sunday is *Weiber Fastnacht*, and women are the absolute rulers on that day. Coming from school one day, I saw a mounted policeman in front of the old Opera House surrounded by at least a dozen young women, all costumed. They danced around this poor (?) fellow and told him he had to dismount and kiss all the girls.

Maybe he was not born in Cologne, and therefore was quite shy. Anyway, the girls hauled him off his horse and he got hugged and kissed by all of them. He was then given permission to get back on his steed, while hundreds of laughing bystanders gave him a thunderous round of applause.

• • •

According to Tony, many German traffic cops were nearly spoiled rotten by extremely appreciative citizens:

In Berlin and Hamburg, traffic at the busiest intersections was controlled by policemen who were specially trained for this sort of work. The officers usually stood on small platforms in the middle of the intersection.

Over the years some of them became very popular with the drivers, who showed their appreciation at Christmastime. Often the platform was covered with hundreds of parcels, with a cop in the middle waving greetings and thanks to his daily customers.

• • •

Tony then hit me with this historical humdinger:

After the Second World War and the fall of the Third Reich, the

German civil services, including the police forces, were "de-Nazified." It was rumoured that quite a few of these jobs went to friends with the proper political connections.

One night, in Cologne, a pedestrian on his way home got robbed on a street where bombings had reduced all the buildings to rubble. As loud as he could, he shouted, "Heil, Hitler!"

Within minutes, several police officers arrived on the scene and arrested the *victim* of the robbery.

"Why did you call 'Heil, Hitler!'?" the poor fellow was asked.

"I tried 'Help! Help!'" he replied, "but nobody came."

• • •

Tony exits with this presentation:

In Switzerland, as in most European countries, it was quite common that at night men following the urgent call of nature relieved themselves on the corners of buildings or on trees. The police in Berne decided to do something about this menace.

One night a tipsy patron leaving his favourite *Gasthaus* felt the urge to dispose of some excess fluid. He spotted someone else across the street who was engaged in doing just that.

He approached a dark corner of a building and was poised to proceed with his intentions when suddenly a policeman approached him and told him to immediately cease and desist.

As the officer started to scribble out a ticket, the accused pointed and said, "Look, there's a fellow doing the same thing over there! Aren't you going to charge him, too?"

"No, sir," replied the cop, "he's our decoy."

• • •

Dennis Connor is a detective with the Organized Crime Task Force of the South Australia Police Department. Back in the mid-1970s, when he was a rookie uniformed policeman, he investigated a situation that still makes him chuckle:

One day, while on a mobile patrol in a suburb of Adelaide, I heard another car being dispatched to the home of a friend of mine concerning an intruder on the premises. I took the assignment because I was in the vicinity. Upon my arrival at the residence, which was directly across the street from a hotel, I was met by my friend's wife, Pam, who was in a mild state of panic.

Pam said she was at home alone when an elderly woman came to the door and asked to use the toilet. Pam let her into the house without thinking and then realized she was quite drunk. She showed her the bathroom and the old dear went in and shut the door.

Pam waited a long time, but the woman did not reappear. The lady of the house then tried to open the door but couldn't. The "guest" had fallen asleep and toppled off the john, blocking the door.

After hearing the story, I went to the bathroom and pushed the door open enough to have a look inside. And there she was, asleep on the floor, track pants and knickers down around her ankles. I pushed the door open and woke her up. I helped her pull up her pants and then escorted her outside to the street. By this time some of the drinkers from the hotel had come over to have a look, as another patrol had attended the scene.

This patrol was crewed by a sergeant and another constable, who were standing on the footpath near where I was attempting to get the old dear's particulars and deciding what to do with her.

As I was speaking to her, she was holding up her track pants. I said, "What am I going to do with you?" and she raised her arms as if to say, "I don't know," when her pants and knickers headed south again, and there she was, naked from the waist down and facing the hotel and the oncoming traffic.

I tried not to break up, but it certainly wasn't easy. I succeeded, though, until the sergeant came over and said to the woman, "I know you're pleased to see me, love, but do you think you could pull up your pants?"

It was impossible not to laugh as the hotel patrons cheered and the oncoming vehicles slowed for a look. The old dear recovered her modesty and we sent her home in a cab.

• • •

Former Windsor, Ontario, policeman Al Porter has many funny cop yarns from both sides of the world's longest undefended border. This story is one of his favourites:

One evening a few years back, a team of Detroit police officers responded to a disturbance call from a bar. When they arrived, the bartender pointed to the rear of the place, where they saw a big man waving his arms and shouting. Destroyed furniture lay all around and there was blood on the floor, indicating that someone had been injured recently. The man was wearing a hooded sweatshirt and sweatpants.

The police team dispatched to the bar consisted of a male officer who was about six feet tall and a female officer who stood maybe five-four. Those in the know say that if you were going to pick one of these two to tangle with, the smart move would be to pick the male. The big man who'd wreaked so much havoc had come to this conclusion, and while he was carefully watching the male officer, the female drew her gun and approached the troublemaker.

As soon as she reached him she grabbed the front of his sweatpants and then stuck the barrel of her 9-mm pistol down the front of his pants. Then in a very sweet voice she asked him if he would like to leave the bar quietly. The man readily agreed, and she kept her gun in place until the three of them had left the bar and the man was ready to enter the police cruiser.

• • •

Constable Jack MacNeill, who's with the RCMP in Charlotte-town, Prince Edward Island, returns to tell us about a madcap runaround he was given one day in the far north:

Working in Frobisher Bay (now called Iqaluit), Northwest Territories, was never dull. The detachment that policed the community of 2,500 regularly processed 1,200 to 1,400 prisoners a year. One summer day about 8:00 a.m., the day-shift members of the force were just finishing their first coffee when an officer's wife called to report that an intoxicated man was trying to strangle a dog that was tied up near the detachment.

I responded in one of the large Suburban police vehicles we used in the north and quickly located the man in question. His advanced state of intoxication was apparent, even from a distance, so I drove up behind him unobserved and was able to back up the vehicle behind him for easier loading.

The man put up very little resistance and he was tucked in the back before he knew what was happening. I then returned to the detachment and entered the cell block through a side door that had been wedged open to improve the quality of the air. Once in the bullpen, the prisoner was instructed to remove the suspenders he was using to hold up his denims.

As the man carried out the instructions to remove his shoes, empty his pockets, provide vital statistics, etc., he became increasingly irritated. As he slipped off his suspenders, his pants fell to his ankles. He muttered, "Screw this," stepped out of his jeans, and staggered to the door and freedom.

Initially I was amused to see this very drunken, bare-assed male, wearing only a T-shirt and socks, make his bid for freedom. However, instead of falling on his face, he banked off a couple of walls and was actually picking up steam and speed. In no time at all he was out the door and running towards the Canadian Broadcasting Company building with a somewhat embarrassed Mountie in pursuit.

During the next few minutes half a dozen motorists and a dozen spectators watching from the CBC windows were entertained by my efforts to apprehend the fugitive. My efforts were successful, but how this exciting event escaped the ever-present eye of a video camera still amazes me. The recapture was inevitable of course, because, as everyone knows, the Mounties always get their man.

I must admit, though, that until then I'd never fully appreciated how much I'd always relied on having clothing *or something else* to hold on to when making arrests.

• • •

Thunder Bay, Ontario, policeman James W. Forbes proved there's another way to grab a hold of a guy — a very effective one. The incident in question arose out of long-standing labour problems that erupted anew outside a medical clinic:

Police were at the scene in their classic role of keepers of the peace. We were attempting to keep strikers back in order to allow clinic management and employees through the line. I was working in plainclothes and was to be an observer. However, when the action started I stopped a man who appeared to be trying to break through the line of police officers from the rear. He was shoved back once and then tried again.

I grabbed the fellow around the neck in a headlock, but he broke free. I grabbed him again in a more secure manner and eventually placed him in a paddy wagon. When he was tried in court I was asked by the prosecutor to describe how I subdued the man. I replied that the second time I took hold of the accused I grabbed him from behind with one arm around his neck and with my other hand I reached through his legs and grabbed his testicles.

During cross-examination, defence counsel asked me to repeat to the court how I grabbed the accused. I did so and was asked, "Did the accused say anything at this time?"

Before I had a chance to reply, Judge Roy Bugowsky cut in

and asked the defence lawyer, "Are you prepared to call medical evidence that a man can say anything coherent while being held in this manner?"

The lawyer said, "No, Your Honour," and the judge then told me not to answer the question. And that was the end of that.

• • •

Fast-thinking and resourceful Hughie V. Brown, formerly of Scotland Yard and now a private eye in Regina, Saskatchewan, has lots of memories of diversions from the boredom and terror of police work. Here's one of his favourites.

What's Up?

The duty officer is in charge of the shift and is usually an inspector or a station sergeant. He has to make all the necessary decisions. When officers are promoted they always get transferred to another station — "A new broom always sweeps clean," as the old saying goes. We had this new duty officer and most of us weren't impressed by him, but he must have had something going for him or he wouldn't have been in that position. A part of the duty officer's work is to patrol around and make sure the officer on the beat is okay and doing his job.

One night shift I was posted to a beat and had teamed up with another officer, a friend of mine. Such pairing was a no-no, and we'd be in trouble if we were caught by the duty officer. We were just approaching a ten-storey building under construction, and we figured we could pass some time if we checked the inside. In we went, cautiously walking through the levels until we reached the top storey.

What a great view we had! I could see most of my beat from up there. This was the place to be, away from the weather and with a bird's-eye view. I looked down. There was the duty officer's car, cruising slowly by. I said to my buddy, "He's probably looking for me."

I picked up a little piece of concrete and let it drop in the direction of his car. A few seconds later I saw his brake lights go on. He then began reversing slowly. I picked up another small piece and let it go over the side. His car came to a stop and just sat there. What's he doing? I wondered. In a short while several other police vehicles pulled up and surrounded the building. Bloody hell, they're going to search it! What are we going to do? Be resourceful, dammit! Think, or we're both in trouble!

My friend and I went down about three levels and hid behind some construction work. We could hear the sound of police boots and voices approaching our level from below. They were up even with us, obviously heading for the top to start a systematic search on the way down. Just when they had passed our level, we left our hiding place and started running up *behind* the other uniformed officers.

"Any sign of anything yet?" I asked no one in particular.

"No, nothing yet," replied an officer, and then he added, "Hughie, you take the east side and we'll take the west."

"Okay, sure," I said, grinning at my buddy.

As we worked our way down we all made a thorough search for a suspicious party or parties but, alas, found absolutely no one. The duty officer was advised that the building was clear, and he drove off rather perplexed.

• • •

Detective Constable Chris Perkins of the Halton Regional Police in Oakville, Ontario, describes a scary adventure he had while serving with Scotland Yard:

It's well known that British police officers are unarmed. I always felt a little safer carrying my issue truncheon, but my partner would constantly leave his in his locker. Late one night we were on regular traffic patrol when a call was broadcast for a patrol car to go to a nearby address — a break and enter in progress, suspects on premises. We were the first unit there, and it was obvious that the premises, a lawyer's office, had been broken into. We cautiously entered the building.

The front door opened to a long flight of stairs to the first-floor offices. Once inside the actual offices we split up, my partner doing one side of the building while I did the other. As I looked around, I could see drawers pulled out and contents spread on the floor. I thought it strange that two small refrigerators had been opened, as well.

It wasn't long before I heard a scream come from across the hall, and with my heart in my mouth I lunged around desks and chairs to reach my colleague, who I suspected was in severe distress. As I entered the room the scream had come from, I was presented with a hilarious sight.

There was my partner holding a male suspect at bay with the cleaner's broom. The suspect had his hands in the air and was holding a large bottle of Glenfiddich whisky. "All right, guv, it's all right . . . no trouble!" he stammered. He pointed to the whisky bottle and asked, "Do you mind?" We watched him down about four inches of the whisky in one gulp. Then he put the bottle down and said, "I'm yours. Let's go."

It seems my partner had been wandering around the offices when he suddenly came across the burglar hiding behind a desk. I think they both messed their trousers about the same time, and the closest weapon my mate could find was the broom, which had been leaning against a wall.

On the way back to the station, with the prisoner in the rear seat (with no cage), the burglar informed us matter-of-factly that he'd recently been paroled after serving seven years for manslaughter. On an earlier B & E, he had tied up an elderly security guard who then died of a heart attack. He told us he felt embarrassed about being caught by a couple of traffic cops.

• • •

Chris Perkins also sent me this reminiscence about a rather historic get-together in London, England.

Did We Leave Anyone Out?

In late 1980 Ronald Reagan was inaugurated as president of the United States. As usual in London, there was an element who felt the need to demonstrate through the streets in protest at this development. Many years earlier there had been a major riot outside the American Embassy in Grovesnor Square, and the police did not want a repeat performance of this.

Hundreds and hundreds of officers were drafted from all over the Metropolitan London area to accompany the march and to ensure that the peace was kept. I was posted to a unit from my station, and we set off for the area in a specially made police bus — ten constables and one sergeant.

When the marchers got to the American Embassy, they staged a sitdown protest and refused to move. The next hour or so got fairly tense as it seemed we would have a major public-order situation on our hands. Eventually police horses were brought in, and the crowd was moved on. At this point we were to return to our bus and prepare for our next deployment.

I was paired with a chap named Jock, and somehow he and I became separated from our group. The police buses start to look strikingly identical when there are thirty or forty of them lined up. Eventually we found our spot and were the brunt of many jokes for having been lost. A suitable punishment was voted on by the group, and Jock and I were ordered off to the underground parking garage of the embassy. The staff there had laid on urns of coffee for the police who were on the demonstration, and we were to secure a tray of coffee for the boys in the bus. As we walked down into the underground, our hearts sank. There was a sea of police helmets and blue uniforms. It seemed the entire force had decided on coffee at the same time. We joined the queue and began our long wait to be served.

Just before we arrived at the front of the line, I could see we were in trouble. Coppers were tilting the urns up to drain the last dregs of coffee. We were going to be out of luck. Everyone who hadn't scored a drink drifted away, and Jock and I were left in the company of a U.S. Marine from the underground gate-guardhouse.

A moment later, a door swung open from across the garage, and another Marine, dressed in full ceremonial kit, sauntered over to us. From somewhere under his tunic he pulled out a bottle of champagne and, much to our surprise, popped the thing right there and then. Jock and I were still holding our plastic-foam coffee cups, and the Marine splashed champers into our cups before we had a chance to protest.

There we were, two bobbies and two Marines, alone in a huge parking garage. The supplier of the champagne lifted his cup and toasted, "To President Reagan." "To President Reagan," we repeated, and drank a toast. The Marine from the guardhouse raised his cup and said, "To freedom!" (This was the same week the Iranian hostages had been released.) "To freedom!" we shouted. "To the British police!" they suggested. "To the British police," we agreed. "To the United States Marine Corps!" we cried. "To the United States Marine Corps," they responded.

We soon emptied the bottle. Before we could slink away, a second bottle appeared from somewhere, and the process was repeated. We toasted everything from the fine English weather to the importing of McDonald's restaurants.

Eventually we arrived back at the police buses, which in the interim had dwindled considerably in number. We sheepishly explained about the long wait and the empty urns, but there was more than one sideways glance at the way our speech and breath had changed.

• • •

Constable Grant Obst of Saskatoon, Saskatchewan, sent me this funny little tale:

The serious problem of substance abuse is not a laughing matter, but I couldn't help chuckling at a predicament my partner and I found ourselves in recently.

We had received a call from a citizen concerned about several young people sniffing solvent in a neighbour's yard. We parked our police vehicle at the end of the block and quietly walked down an alley to a point where we were able to observe the people involved.

Once establishing the legitimacy of the complaint, we approached the teenagers. One young man tried to conceal a rather large can of lacquer thinner in his pants. Upon questioning him as to the ownership of the thinner, it became obvious that no one knew who the stuff belonged to. At that point it became found property, which I retained. The youths were lectured on the hazards of substance abuse and sent on their way.

As my partner and I, along with our container of thinner, started down the alley towards our car, a lady opened her back gate, entered the alley and deposited a bag in a trash bin. When she spotted us and our can, she casually inquired, "Don't you guys do doughnuts anymore?"

• • •

Betty Whiddington, of New York City, recalls a dandy yarn she learned from her father, Charles C. Middlebro', who was the Crown Attorney in Owen Sound, Ontario, in the fifties and sixties:

One of my father's favourite stories happened in the early fifties and concerned two tramps who lived near a quarry in the village of Williamsford. They were a great trial to the local police because they were always drunk and getting into fights and generally making nuisances of themselves.

One night they got spectacularly drunk and got into a fight, and one of them took the bottle and hit the other one over the head and killed him. In his drunken state he heaved the body into the quarry and passed out. When he came to, he felt terrible in every sense of the word and took himself to the local police station where he tried to explain the story to the bored, disbelieving, and generally fed-up cop, who eventually agreed to go and take a look.

As he was going out the door, the policeman said, "Now, listen here, Bert, if there's no body in that quarry, you're in big trouble!"

• • •

Laughter can erupt even in tragic circumstances. Just ask Detective Kenneth A. "Mac" MacKenzie, a thirty-year veteran with the state police in Hastings, Victoria, Australia.

One day in the 1980s, Mac was dispatched to an address where, minutes earlier, a man had blown his brains out with a shotgun. He and another policeman stood guard in the room where this had happened, and it wasn't long before a morbid mob of the deceased's relatives appeared on the scene.

"They demanded they be allowed to enter the room to see the devastation," Mac said in a letter to me. "Naturally, such a request was denied. As can be expected, a great deal of wailing and gnashing of teeth was occurring amongst the relatives, and the dead man's brother was obviously embarrassed by their antics and assumed that my colleague and I were, too. He stayed with us to ease our perceived embarrassment and chatted about his recently deceased brother. Then he broke the tension with a comment that will stay with me forever.

"'I just can't understand what my brother was thinking about,' he said. 'You know, he's never done anything like this before.'"

225

• • •

A while ago, the editor of San Diego's police newsletter wrote this shocking piece entitled "Hell Hath No Fury":

If any of you are playing kissie face with more than one lady, you might do well to heed the Christmas Eve visit received by a hapless Romeo who loved and lost.

Lady #1 appeared at Romeo's residence, clad only in a teddy and trenchcoat, and whispered that she had always wanted to "do it" in an office. Intrigued with the idea, Romeo bundled her off to his office.

Once inside, Lady #1 brought out some silken scarves and suggested that it might be fun to tie him up with them, just a little bit. Once he was trussed up, Lady #1 went to the door and let someone else in. Nope, it wasn't Santa. It was Lady #2, Romeo's alleged ex-girlfriend with an electronic stun gun that's known as a Taser.

The two ladies proceeded to make a human Christmas tree out of Romeo by zapping him ten to fifteen times with the Taser in an especially sensitive portion of his anatomy. That's what happens to bad little Romeos who hit on two Juliets at the same time. Especially when the two Juliets are friends and figure out what he's up to.

Yes, the ladies were arrested. But somehow, I'd bet that they were laughing all the way to the station.

• • •

Constable William D. Mutch, of the Niagara Regional Police Service, has been involved in many humorous situations in his seventeen years as a cop. Here's his report on one of them:

During the summer we get all sorts of tourists in Niagara Falls, Ontario. Some get into the most amazing predicaments. I got an assistance call from one of the motels on Lundy's Lane, our "strip." The dispatcher wouldn't give me any details over the air, and I was riding a motorcycle, so I didn't have a computer to tell me what was going on.

When I got there, I went up to the room and knocked. The door opened about two inches, and the guy standing behind it practically dragged me into the room. The first thing I noticed was a girl on the bed with a sheet pulled right up to her chin. She looked like she weighed about 250 pounds. The guy said, "Can you help us? We can't get them off."

It turned out they had gone to the sex shop next door, bought a pair of handcuffs, put them on the girl, had their fun, then, when they went to get the cuffs off, they broke both keys.

I said to the girl, "Let's see the cuffs." She managed to get them out from under the sheet and keep her modesty.

I saw right away that they were cheap novelty cuffs and that my key wouldn't fit. I also figured I could break them easily if I had a screwdriver or knife, which I did. However, I looked at the cuffs and said, "My key won't fit those, I'm afraid. I guess the only thing is to call the fire department." Both started pleading with me not to do that, and I finally gave in.

I got out my Swiss army knife, popped out the screwdriver, and managed to pry the cuffs apart in a minute or so. It wasn't easy because they had put about a quart of hand lotion on the girl's wrists to try to slide the cuffs off. Well, I finally got her out of them, and the lovebirds were both very grateful. I'm just glad it wasn't a chastity belt they were fooling around with.

• • •

Captain Don Strand of the Iowa City Police Department wrote:

Here's a true story concerning an arrest made by one of my sergeants, who responded to a routine disturbance call. Upon his arrival he was able to determine the cause of the disturbance and told the suspect he was under arrest and ordered him to get into the squad car.

The man protested, "You can't arrest me, I'm schizophrenic." The sergeant didn't hesitate for a moment and said, "Okay, you're *both* under arrest. Get in the car."

• • •

Jay Johnson, a policeman in the town of North East, Maryland, sent me a note recently about a rather unusual request:

Earlier today, I responded to a "malicious destruction of property" call following a storm. I had to tell the victim that I didn't care what his insurance company said about "act of God," I would not take a report on the tree sticking through his car listing God as a "suspect."

• • •

Radio operators, or dispatchers, play extremely important roles in police work everywhere. Cheryl Ann Pratt is a dispatcher in the busy southeastern Utah tourist town of Moab, located in a spectacular area of red rocks, desert, the La Sal Mountains, and the Colorado River.

For the past eight years Cheryl has jotted down hundreds of moronic inquiries in a notebook, which she says gets funnier by the day. Here are some of the wackier queries she's handled:

• I'd like to rent a Jeep and hire a guide for in the mountains. Could you handle these arrangements for me since you are a public servant?

• I just want to report that there are two deer in my front yard. Will you send someone over to chase them out of my yard?

• Could you please tell me the name of the motel in Bluff that we made our reservations at?

• I'm meeting my family in Price and I wondered if you knew

the name of the restaurant we're meeting at since I forgot.

• Operator, ring back on my line to see if it works. I'm having problems with it.

• My car was broken down, and now I have it running again. I'm now headed to Price from Moab and I just know my car will die again. Could you please have a trooper follow me from Moab to Price in case it does?

• My husband has gas and he can't quit farting. Can you give us directions to the hospital?

• There's a woman riding the train nude. We need assistance in removing her. (This from an Amtrack dispatcher).

• We wish you a merry Christmas and a happy new year. (It was July 29.)

• My wife is downtown and my son smashed his pee-pee with the potty lid. His pee-pee is now black. Please have someone watch for my wife — I really want her to come home now.

• I need two Tylenols. Could you get those for me?

• Could you help me please? My contact lenses are stuck in my eyes and I can't get them out.

• How do I dial the operator?

• How much water is flowing in the Colorado River?

• If the temperature in Moab is 68, does that mean there's snow on the ground?

• Can you tell me what streets are flooded in Missouri?

• Can you tell me if the houses in Price, Utah, are sinking because they're built on top of coal mines?

• I received information three days ago that will rewrite the history of Adolf Hitler. I need to talk to the sheriff as soon as possible.

• We've had a couple of drinks and don't want to drive. However, we want to go out to the Sportsman's Bar. Would you have an officer pick us up, take us to the Sportsman's, then take us back when we're finished partying?

• • •

And speaking of police dispatchers . . .

"There are a lot of crazies out there," says Shannon MacDonald of Toronto, who used to be a 911 operator with the Edmonton, Alberta, police force. "The number of calls they get from people convinced they're being monitored and/or observed by aliens from outer space is, well, crazy.

"Somewhere along the line, a clever copper conceived of a way to deal with these poor paranoid souls. You tell them to cover their ceilings with tin foil — shiny side up, of course — because this deflects the alien 'rays.'

"A few years ago, a creative thinker at the Edmonton police headquarters added a new twist," Shannon continues. "He had a caller who refused to be satisfied with the foil on the ceiling, and so he advised the man to also line his hat with tin foil. When that still wasn't quite enough, he suggested that a headband worn with a green dot centre front would do the trick. He added that it worked for the officers working on the computers. At last the caller was satisfied."

A few days later, a man wearing a foil-lined cap and green-dotted headband came into police headquarters. He said the hat and dot had worked such wonders the aliens could no longer get at him. He was overjoyed and wanted to personally thank the operator who'd given him such wonderful advice.

"Uh-oh, this required quick action," recalls Shannon MacDonald. "The sergeant, who'd heard the story about this guy, asked him if he'd mind waiting a few minutes, then disappeared into the radio room. When the sergeant reappeared and ushered the man in, all the officers at the computers were hard at work — and every head sported a headband with a bright green dot smack-dab in the middle."

• • •

"Vengeance is mine," saith the Lord. Well . . .

Retired police seargeant Samuel Hill, of Coleraine, Northern Ireland, sent me this splendid story about a citizen who was on the outs with a local cop, and vice versa:

In the nearby town of Ballymoney, where I served for five years, a clergyman rang a sergeant of police to inform him that he'd found a dead donkey on his property.

The sergeant said, "But sure it's your duty to bury the dead?" and the man of cloth replied, "but it's also my duty to notify the next of kin."

• • •

If France decided to recast its laws in biblical form, a heart-breaking — and wallet-breaking — commandment would likely be one that reads as follows: Thou shalt not jostle a cop.

My remark is prompted by a darkly comical story I received recently in a letter from Jean François Nouhet, an inspector of police in the town of St. Cyr L'école, near Paris. It had to do with the sad fix a man found himself in when charged under a brand-new law. As the story unfolds, you can almost hear Dickens's Beadle Bumble snorting, "The law is a ass, a idiot."

In 1994 a man suspected of stealing a pump from an aquar-ium ignored several letters asking him to come to the police station to answer questions at a "preliminary inquiry." So, invoking a recently enacted law that had yet to be used, Inspector Nouhet and two other gendarmes went to the man's house and lugged him off to jail, where he'd remain "in police custody" pending the outcome of an investigation.

Before heading off to the hoosegow, the alleged culprit protested vehemently to the police that he'd had nothing to do with the theft, and he added that that was why he hadn't responded to their invitations. As the man's anger increased, Inspector Nouhet writes, "he jostled one of my colleagues." As

231

a result of this belligerent behaviour, he says, "the other Inspector and I were copiously insulted."

Jostling is a big no-no in French police circles, it seems.

"By jostling the officer the guy made himself guilty of 'rebellion and outrage' towards the agents of the police force, and he was officially charged with such a crime," the inspector advises. "And it was also because of his rebellious behaviour that we had to use force to immobilize him. He was manacled and dragged out of his home and then loaded into our car. We came back to the police station, where at last the man could be heard on the matter of the alleged theft of the pump."

With the hapless suspect safely parked in prison, police proceeded with the investigation, which took several days of hard sleuthing by Inspector Nouhet and Company.

"At the end of our investigation," the inspector reports, "it appeared that our guy had nothing to do with the theft of the pump. His innocence was confirmed — thanks to a confrontation with the victim, who didn't recognize him. The true perpetrator had fled the scene in a car that appeared to have been registered in the name of the man we later put in custody, but we discovered it had been falsely registered and the real crook had also used our guy's licence plate."

That was the good news. The bad news was as follows:

"Our guy," writes the inspector, "was found guilty on the rebellion charge and ordered to pay a fine of 2,000 francs." (About $650 in Canadian funds.)

Inspector Nouhet, who strongly dislikes the wording of the new law he brought into play, then stated, "Your readers will be stupefied to know that this man was condemned on a fact [jostling a cop] that was a result of his expression of injustice."

So what should one do, storm the Bastille? Maybe in time the jostler will be able to laugh about what he's been through. Laughter often is a delayed reaction. As James Thurber said, "Humour is emotional chaos remembered in tranquillity."

• • •

Fredericton, New Brunswick, established in 1785 and named after Frederick, son of King George III, has one of the oldest organized police departments in Canada.

There were only two officers in the force that sprang into being on June 27, 1851, three years after the town of Fredericton became a city of only 2,000 souls. (It's around 50,000 now.) It wasn't until twenty-two years later, in 1873, that the North-West Mounted Police — later renamed the Royal Canadian Mounted Police — galloped proudly onto the scene.

Now, thanks to the diligent research of Inspector Eric Fiander and Sergeant Eric Carr, veterans of the Fredericton police force who spent many long hours in the New Brunswick Archives, mounds of humorous material — humorous, that is, in retrospect — that showed what it was like to be a Fredericton cop more than a century ago have been unearthed.

These policemen of yesteryear dealt with situations that required strength or resourcefulness or compassion or all three — pretty much the way it is with today's cops. Also, like today's cops, many of the things they had to do — or perhaps what they had to do *without* — produced results that were really quite laughable. Here are a few:

In January 1859, nearly eight years after the police force was formed, a grand jury was selected to examine and report on the condition of the Fredericton police lockup. One of the jury's recommendations was "to see and to supply those prisoners who have neither friends nor means to provide the same with at least occasional changes in inner apparel, and this we cannot too strongly urge as one prisoner has been confined without a change [of underwear] since last June."

• • •

Fredericton Police Court was a quite busy in the early 1870s. Here are some of the illicit activities the court dealt with:

• July 26, 1871 — James McCormack, vagrancy; fined $3.00. Ordered escorted to city line by police and to leave the city.

• August 26, 1871 — John McCarty, encumbering streets; fined $1.20.

• August 27, 1871 — John McCarty, encumbering streets; fined $4.80.

• November 30, 1871 — John Foley, cruelty to animals, dragging a cow by the horns while down on her side across the river on the ice; fined $5.00.

• November 10, 1872 — Catherine Whitmichael, allowing cows to run at large; fined $1.70.

• November 10, 1872 — Thomas Rodgers, shouting on Sunday; fined $5.50.

• November 10, 1872 — James Rodgers, shouting on Sunday; fined $2.50.

• July 27, 1873 — Thomas Rodgers, causing frequent disturbances; one month in jail.

• July 27, 1873 — Thomas Rodgers, stealing a bottle of brandy; three months in jail.

Cussin' was a constant concern of the authorities, and on November 10, 1872, the *New Brunswick Reporter* tersely — and colourfully — told its readers: "The police arraigned a young ruffian today for profanity. 'It is too bad that the very air we breathe should be made pestilential with the vapours of oaths and blasphemies,' laments Policeman Woodward."

• • •

Police work is often thankless. No one knew it better than this nineteenth-century Fredericton copper. "Policeman Moxon retired from the police force on Friday," read a newspaper report published November 5, 1873. "He has shown himself a faithful and zealous officer. A motion before City Council to thank him publicly for his tireless years of service was defeated."

• • •

Oh, happy day! On October 4, 1892, all four Fredericton cops realized they were starting to get some of the recognition they so richly deserved. That was the historic day that the skinflint City Council voted to give the Fredericton Police Department permission to "procure a pair of handcuffs." A mere forty-one years after entering the rough-and-tumble, dangerous business of hauling criminals off to jail, they finally had a pair of handcuffs they could take turns using.

But that was just the start of their good fortune. The coppers were on a roll!

On May 2, 1893, City Council decreed, "The Police Department is given leave to purchase a cord of hardwood for the police office this winter. The City Treasurer advances two dollars to Sergeant Phillips for this."

And then, as if all that largesse weren't enough, on August 4, 1894, Council tossed money around wildly again, this time ruling, "The Police Department is given permission to purchase a secure door for the cell." The gendarmes were beside themselves with joy. After a paltry forty-three years they were getting a cell door that would *lock*!

Well, you can imagine how thrilled the cops were when, once again, the City Fathers fell into their arms. On September 3, 1895, only nineteen years after Mr. A.G. Bell invented the contraption, Fredericton City Council proclaimed, "The Police Department is given permission to get a telephone."

"What will the police get next?" folks asked all over town.

The four policemen let it be known that they sure could use a rubber raincoat — each.

On November 6, 1895, City Council voted as follows:

"Moved that Council buy four rubber raincoats for use by the police officers while on duty in inclement weather. Motion defeated."

Well, as the old baseball saying goes, "You win some, you lose some, and some are rained out."

• • •

The Fredericton Police Department has come a long way in the past century. "It's considered one of the most progressive police forces in Atlantic Canada," boasts researcher extraordinaire Inspector Eric Fiander, "and it's a pioneer in community-based policing and the testing of new technology. We have ninety-eight police officers now, and in addition to our headquarters, we have four neighbourhood offices, two storefront offices, and a recreational vehicle that's used as a mobile office."

After heaping further praise on the force's modern facilities and vast fleet of vehicles, Fiander adds with a grin, "We have lots of telephones and raincoats, and our officers have at least one pair of handcuffs — *each*."

• • •

In 1984 lawyer Douglas Schofield exchanged his prosecutor's job in Kelowna, British Columbia, for the same sort of employment in Hamilton, Bermuda. Years later he sent me the complete lowdown on a wacky case he'd looked into that was tried in his adopted city back in the late 1970s:

The Crown was prosecuting a local malefactor for importation of a controlled drug. The only hard evidence of identity was a single fingerprint, found on the *inner* surface of the material the drugs were packaged in.

A member of the Bermuda Police Scenes-of-Crime Office attended before the Supreme Court judge and jury to testify to the fingerprint identification. Bermuda adheres to British Home Office policy on fingerprints: a minimum of sixteen points of identical ridge characteristics must be found before an officer will be permitted to make a positive identification in court.

The policeman who is to testify always prepares a fingerprint chart. It consists of side-by-side photographic enlargements of the "questioned" and "known" prints, with the various points of identification highlighted and numbered.

The police officer testified before judge and jury, filed his chart, and concluded by saying that the fingerprint on the packaging was definitely made by a digit of the defendant "and by no other person." Defence counsel's cross-examination was not at all thorough or effective. Other circumstantial evidence implicating the prisoner was led by the Crown, but it, too, was not very compelling. Still, a conviction seemed likely.

It was not to be. To the astonishment of everyone, including the defence counsel, the jury acquitted. The Scenes-of-Crime officer was incensed. He brooded over the insult for days.

One evening, while off duty and passing the time in a local watering hole, he spotted a familiar face. Fortified by a few drinks, he approached the ex-foreman of the recalcitrant jury.

The conversation went like this:

POLICEMAN: See here, weren't you on a jury last week?

JUROR: Yeah.

POLICEMAN: Do you remember me?

JUROR: Sure — you're that fingerprint guy.

POLICEMAN: Yes. What I want to know is why you people found the accused not guilty. We found his fingerprint *inside* the wrappings on the drugs! There was no explanation as to how it got there! How could you let him off?

JUROR: Hell, you cops must think juries are stupid. We looked at your pretty chart. In fact, we spent a lot of time studying it in the jury room. But we also sat in that courtroom for a week looking at that defendant. No way, man! No way!

POLICEMAN: No way? Whaddaya mean, no way?

JUROR: Just no way his fingers were that big! *No way!*

237

• • •

Retired businessman Russell D. Wallace, of Halifax, Nova Scotia, had a brief career as a cop, serving with the RCMP in New Glasgow, Nova Scotia, between 1943 and 1946. He has many humorous memories of those years, and here's one of them:

One day, while driving a wino to jail, I asked him what he'd been drinking to get arrested and he said shoe polish. As a joke, I asked if it had been black or brown, and he said he always drank the black as the brown upset his stomach.

• • •

It's amazing how perceptive some police bigwigs are in sizing up situations they encounter in the execution of their duties. Consider, for example, this wee item that appeared a few years ago in the famous Edinburgh newspaper, *The Scotsman.*

He'll Make Chief One Day

There were 26 people there, 22 men and four women, drinking beer and spirits. Four full 11-gallon canisters of beer, five empty ones, one part full, 415 cans of pale ale and lager, 22 partly full cans, 68 empty cans, and several dozen beer and spirit glasses were found.

"I came to the conclusion that this was a place used for drinking," said the Inspector.

• • •

And take a squint at this terribly terse production, which appeared in the London, England, *Sunday Express.*

Love Conquers All

Police said the toll rose to eight dead last night — five women and three men, including the gunman — and 11 injured, three critically.

"It looks like a lovers' tiff," said a detective.

• • •

An Edmonton cop who wishes to remain anonymous wrote to tell me about a glamorous mission he was given one memorable evening early in his career. He'd been assigned to "work in the cells," an undefined pleasure that had previously eluded him. Here, in his own words, is what happened:

The cell-block sergeant was quick to inform me that I had drawn a special assignment. I hadn't been on the job long, but I'd been on long enough to know not to volunteer for anything and to be leery of any and all "special assignments."

The drug squad had arrested a man they suspected of swallowing a bundle of heroin. They felt the drug had been concealed in a balloon or condom and were anxious to retrieve it. A danger existed that the package could burst, so the prisoner would have to be kept under constant observation. He was placed in a small holding room with a window and instructed to advise me if and when he felt the call of nature.

As I sat with my tools, consisting of a metal pail, a pair of rubber gloves, and a popsicle stick, I couldn't help wondering why cops never have to put up with this sort of thing.

I also recalled a story my father told me about a special assignment that had come to his attention when he was in the air force. Apparently the commanding officer confronted the enlisted men and asked if any of them were interested in music. When six of them said they were, they were ordered to move a piano.

Anyway, as the shift wore on I remember wishing a severe case of irregularity on the fellow in the room. I thought I would receive my wish, but with approximately three-quarters of an hour left in my shift the dreaded signal came.

I directed the prisoner into the back, where he did his business into the pail. With great reluctance, I began my investigation. It was an extensive one, too, but it turned up only a few salmon bones.

About two weeks later, dressed in civilian duds, I went to lunch in a downtown restaurant. After beginning my meal I looked across the crowded room and saw the fellow I'd "investigated" so thoroughly. There was no conversation between us, but we both burst out laughing.

Come to think of it, there was absolutely no mention of this sort of work in the police recruiting posters.

• • •

A similar situation arose in Ontario about fifteen years ago. A Toronto man, charged with possession of drugs for the purpose of trafficking, asked to be released on bail. It was alleged that he'd swallowed several condoms full of hashish oil and, naturally, the authorities didn't want him to get away on them until they'd had a chance to recover the evidence.

The prosecutor and defence lawyer agreed that the accused should be released on bail, but not until he'd had three bona fide bowel movements.

Each of these momentous events would be closely monitored, the court was advised. All movements were to be deposited in a chamber pot under the scrutiny of a member of the Royal Canadian Mounted Police, and it was the duty of this lucky fellow to check each movement "minutely." He could hardly wait to plunge into action.

The judge asked if the accused agreed to this procedure, and defence counsel said he did. Then the judge asked the lawyer, "Do you realize what you're doing to that poor Mountie?"

"What do you mean, Your Honour?" counsel inquired.

"You're turning him into a stool pigeon," replied the judge.

P.S.

I'm hard at work on a sequel to this book, and I'd love to receive scads of funny true tales pertaining to the world of cops. If you have any such stories, hailing from anywhere on this planet, please fire them off to me by letter, fax, or tape, at either of the addresses shown below.

As in the past, the names of donors whose anecdotes are accepted for publication will be preserved for posterity in the honour roll at the back of the book.

And please note (he says modestly) that I can be persuaded to convulse audiences with tales from the courtroom and/or cop shop. You might have seen my motto somewhere: "Have tongue, will travel."

Send your stories and speaking inquiries to:

Peter V. MacDonald
555-18th Avenue
Hanover, Ontario
Canada N4N 3B2
Fax/phone: (519) 364-3344

Or, if you prefer, mail them to:
Peter V. MacDonald
c/o General Distribution Services
85 River Rock Drive, #202
Buffalo, New York 14207 U.S.A.

Contributors

Constable Justine Adamek, Federal Police, Canberra, Australia
Deputy Chief Garney Arcand, Bellevue, Washington, U.S.A.
Constable Stuart Armstrong, Oakville, Ontario, Canada
F. V. Arul, Insp. Gen. of Police (Ret.),Egmore, Madras, India

Kaye Baker, Bongaree, Bribie Island, Queensland, Australia
Constable Shelley Ballard, Saskatoon, Saskatchewan, Canada
Noela A. Bamford, Regina, Saskatchewan, Canada
Charles M. Bauer, Ottawa, Ontario, Canada
Ronald Berry, Chatsworth, Ontario, Canada
Corporal Andrew Black, Royal Canadian Mounted Police,
   Ottawa, Ontario, Canada
Officer Brett Blacker, Edgewater, Maryland, U.S.A.
Chief Jerry Bledsoe, Chaffee, Missouri, U.S.A.
Chris Boyer, Kitchener, Ontario, Canada
Hugh V. Brown, Regina, Saskatchewan, Canada
Jack Burton, Lindsay, Ontario, Canada

Constable George Cameron, Summerside, Prince Edward
   Island, Canada
Sergeant Eric Carr, Fredericton, New Brunswick, Canada
Donatas Z. Cernius, London, Ontario, Canada
Constable Duncan Chisholm, Royal Canadian Mounted Police,
   Deer Lake, Newfoundland, Canada

Detective Patrick J. Cleary, Cork, Ireland
Detective Dennis Connor, Adelaide, South Australia, Australia
James E. Crawford, Scarborough, Ontario, Canada

Superintendent Gary Crowell, Peel Regional Police, Brampton, Ontario, Canada

Sergeant Gary Dale, Port Elgin, Ontario, Canada
Detective Terry L. Davis, Lemoore, California, U.S.A.
Officer Sunshine Dayton, New York, New York, U.S.A.
Mike DiMiceli, Citrus Heights, California, U.S.A.
Sergeant John P. Duffy, Archivist, Police Headquarters, Dublin, Ireland

Sergeant Keith Edwards, Crayford, Kent, England

Brian R. Farmer, Walkerton, Ontario, Canada
Constable Greg Ferguson, Royal Canadian Mounted Police, Hampton, New Brunswick, Canada
Inspector Eric Fiander, Fredericton, New Brunswick, Canada
Judge Stewart Fisher, Brampton, Ontario, Canada
James W. Forbes, Thunder Bay, Ontario, Canada

George Gamester, *Toronto Star*, Toronto, Ontario, Canada
Alex Goldie, Soldiers Cove, Nova Scotia, Canada
John Golightly, Stonehaven, Kincardineshire, Scotland
Jack Gordon, Hanover, Ontario, Canada
Officer Michael L. Grant, St. Johnsbury, Vermont, U.S.A.
Lawrence Greenspon, Ottawa, Ontario, Canada
Lieutenant Roger A. Gross, Fairfax Station, Virginia, U.S.A.
Judge Harold Gyles, Winnipeg, Manitoba, Canada

Staff-Sergeant Steve Hibbard, Cambridge, Ontario, Canada
Samuel Hill, Coleraine, Northern Ireland
Lewis Howells, Pontllanfraith, Blackwood, Gwent, Wales
Constable Brian Jack, Royal Canadian Mounted Police, Powerview, Manitoba, Canada
Dave Jacobs, Dartmouth, Nova Scotia, Canada

Officer Jay Johnson, North East, Maryland, U.S.A.

Jennifer M. Kelly, Santry, Dublin, Ireland
Sergeant Dorothy Kern, San Diego, California, U.S.A
Tony Krings, Scarborough, Ontario, Canada

Robert J. Lane, Shellbrook, Saskatchewan, Canada
Sidney Laufer, Toronto, Ontario, Canada
Michael J. Laurie, St. John's, Newfoundland, Canada
Sergeant Jim Liles, Covington, Kentucky, U.S.A.
Judge Spyros D. Loukidelis, Sudbury, Ontario, Canada
Morley S. Lymburner, Markham, Ontario, Canada

Alan H. MacDonald, Calgary, Alberta, Canada
Michael J. MacDonald, Manly, New South Wales, Australia
Shannon MacDonald, Toronto, Ontario, Canada
John MacIntyre, Sydney, Nova Scotia, Canada
Detective Kenneth A. MacKenzie, Hastings, Victoria, Australia
Constable Jack MacNeill, Royal Canadian Mounted Police,
    Charlottetown, Prince Edward Island, Canada
David L. Makin, Kanata, Ontario, Canada
Constable Andrew Maksymchuk, Ontario Provincial Police,
    Sudbury, Ontario, Canada
Sergeant Patrick A. McBride, Matsqui, British Columbia, Canada
Chief Justice Allan McEachern, Vancouver, British Columbia,
    Canada
Robert B. McGee, Toronto, Ontario, Canada
Staff-Sergeant Michael McGinn, Timmins, Ontario, Canada
Alex McKay, Portsoy, Banff, Scotland
William M. McGrath, Acton, Ontario, Canada
Bob and Willa McLean, Kitchener, Ontlario, Canada
Annette McLoughlin, Dundruon, Dublin, Ireland
Ed McPhail, Milton, Ontario, Canada
Athol J. Montague, Launceston, Tasmania, Australia

David N. Muise, Sydney, Nova Scotia, Canada
Donald G. Mungham, Orillia, Ontario, Canada
Lietenant-Colonel D. Brian Murphy, Ottawa, Ontario, Canada
Constable William D. Mutch, Niagara Regional Police Service,
Niagara Falls, Ontario, Canada

Jean Francois Nouhet, Saint Cyr L'école, France

Dale Obermeyer, Ancaster, Ontario, Canada
Constable Grant R. Obst, Saskatoon, Saskatchewan, Canada

Kathleen Park, Thornbury, North Bristol, England
Joseph T. Parsons, Royal Canadian Mounted Police (ret.),
Reg. # 10851
Lois Pearce, Chatham, Ontario, Canada
Detective-Constable Chris Perkins, Oakville, Ontario, Canada
Denis Perkins, Waterloo, Ontario, Canada
Al Porter, Detroit, Michigan, U.S.A.
Constable John Potts, Ontario Provincial Police, Walkerton,
Ontario, Canada
Cheryl Ann Pratt, Moab, Utah, U.S.A.
Maggie Preston, Toronto, Ontario, Canada
Mr. Justice Stuart S. Purvis, Edmonton, Alberta, Canada

Echo Railton, Port Colborne, Ontario, Canada
Prof. S. Venugopal Rao, Andhra Pradesh Police Academy,
Hyderabad, India
Ingrid Ratz, Winnipeg, Manitoba, Canada
Nora Reid, Port Colborne, Ontario, Canada
Delphine Richards, Cysgod-Y-Castell, Dryslwyn, Carmarthen,
Dyfed, Wales
J.R. Richards, Brecon, Powys LD3 7NE, Wales
Sergeant Brian Rogers, Royal Canadian Mounted Police,
Regina, Saskatchewan, Canada

Officer Kirk J. Roncskevitz, Nashville, Tennessee, U.S.A.
Judge Dwayne Rowe, Sidney, British Columbia, Canada

Constable Fred Sauve, Ontario Provincial Police, North Bay,
Ontario, Canada
Douglas Schofield, Hamilton, Bermuda
Constable Michele Smith, Port Germein, South Australia,
Australia
Sergeant Denis M. Stanes, Victoria State Police, Korumburra,
Victoria, Australia
Steve Stirling, Port Alberni, British Columbia, Canada
Captain Don Strand, Iowa City, Iowa, U.S.A.
Judge Hazen Strange, Oromocto, New Brunswick, Canada
Constable John Stuckey, Springwood, New South Wales,
Australia

Gwyn "Jocko" Thomas, North York, Ontario, Canada
Constable Mark Tregellas, Victoria State Police, Portland,
Victoria, Australia

Constable Kevin Wakeford, Edmonton, Alberta, Canada
Russell D. Wallace, Halifax, Nova Scotia, Canada
A. "Scotty" Wallace, Midland, Ontario, Canada
Constable Kevin Washnuk, Ontario Provincial Police,
Walkerton, Ontario, Canada
Jack Webster, Metropolitan Police Headquarters, Toronto,
Ontario, Canada
Sergeant Les Weir, Ontario Provincial Police, Petrolia, Ontario,
Canada
Betty Whiddington, New York, New York, U.S.A.
A.J. (Jack) While, Winnipeg, Manitoba, Canada
Jack White, Kamloops, British Columbia, Canada
Geeske C. Williams, R.R. 1, Port Hastings, Nova Scotia,
Canada